To Caroline –

Thanks for waitressing at the party.

Here's hoping you have a good & valuable time in Glasgow. Good luck for the drama course and keep an open mind, absorb the 'happenings' and I'm sure you'll meet a wider range of people – so be happy!

all my love

Joe xxx.

P.S. Don't just read the chapters about nightlife & arts – the rest of it, including the political bit is worth knowing. I wish I knew more about Edinburgh!

Glasgow Herald Book of

GLASGOW

THE GLASGOW
HERALD
BOOK OF
GLASGOW

MAINSTREAM
PUBLISHING

IN CONJUNCTION WITH
THE GLASGOW HERALD

All rights reserved
First published in Great Britain 1989 by
MAINSTREAM PUBLISHING COMPANY
(EDINBURGH) LTD
7 Albany Street
Edinburgh EH1 3UG
ISBN 1 85158 234 7 (cloth)

British Library Cataloguing in Publication Data
The Glasgow Herald book of Glasgow.
  1. Scotland. Strathclyde Region. Glasgow, history
  I. Kemp, A.
  941.4'43

ISBN 1-85158-234-7

Design and finished artwork by
James Hutcheson and Paul Keir

Typeset in 10/11pt Sabon by Hewer Text, Edinburgh
Printed in Great Britain by Butler and Tanner Ltd, Frome

Contents

To Uncle George

Foreword

THIS BOOK REPRESENTS AN UNUSUAL UNDERTAKING. ANTHOLOGIES OF material already published in newspapers are perfectly commonplace but an original collection by writers in one stable is rare. (I use the word rare in its normal English sense but also with its colloquial Scots meaning of something that is very enjoyable and nice, perhaps the best available translation of the German word *gemütlich*.) As the Editor of the *Glasgow Herald*, I am very proud of my stable and the richness of its resources: to the string of writers here paraded I could have added numerous others.

From time to time people advise me that the *Herald* should drop Glasgow from its title. This has never appealed to me at all. This is not only because it is a venerable title. It also enjoys a reputation for excellence and authority throughout the newspaper world. If there ever was an argument for dropping it, that case is much diminished by Glasgow's emergence as a city not just of the past but also of the future. In 1990, as all the world surely now knows, the city is European City of Culture, and this book is a kind of celebration of the *Herald*'s home town, a city that maybe lost its way for a while but never lost its heart or its hope.

Without the inspiration of Mainstream, and its partners Bill Campbell and Peter MacKenzie, we would never have been prodded into producing this book. Without our 'trainer', Ronnie Anderson (the *Herald*'s Executive Editor), the runners would never have got out of the stable. Without the support of our Managing Director, Ian J. Irvine, CA, they would have fallen at the first fence. My sincere thanks to them all.

Arnold Kemp

ARNOLD KEMP

Introduction

A CITY IS A SERIES OF VILLAGES. IF YOU FLY IN TO GLASGOW AT NIGHT you can see them there, bright clusters linked by chains of light, the gleam of the river in the shadows. But the villages of the city have more than a mere physical or topographical meaning. Glasgow is composed of vocational or professional communities which are themselves villages with discrete and self-regulating lives. Politicians lurk in the marbled splendour of the City Chambers, business types dine in numerous clubs and sodalities, lawyers in their gowns cluster like crows at the criminal courts (an industry that knows no recession) or contest the market in house purchase with an army of estate agents. And although the City Chambers kicks with its left and the Trades House with its right, this cellular city is strongly bonded into a body corporate in which the things that unite are more important than those that divide. The great unifying agent is love, although that love can seem close to hate. Bertrand Russell said that few people can be happy unless they hate some other person, nation or creed. The rivalries of Glasgow, particularly on the football field, have made the satisfaction of that need systematic and institutionalised. The chants of the terracing float upwards like poison gas but, distressing as they are to those of sensibility and liberal sentiment, they seem to arise from a process as natural and malodorous as the fermentation of a dung heap. Yet, just as from decay comes new life in nature, so too, amid rivalries rooted in old fears and grievances, there is to be found a transcending love of Glasgow. The true-blue businessman may harbour an ideological distaste for the Labour councillor but sits down with him cheerfully enough in the common interest.

When I first came to Glasgow from Edinburgh eight years ago – probably the biggest cultural switch any Scotsman may be required to make without first going furth of the country – I took a taxi to a restaurant in Hope Street. 'Is that Hope and Bath?' the driver inquired. It was another intimation that the American influence in Glasgow is strong. It expresses itself not only in borrowed usage, but also in the very grid of the city centre, which is more North American in character than any other town in the United Kingdom. Within the rectangle between George Square in the east and Blythswood in the west there is, admittedly in miniature, that right-angled pattern of avenues and streets so typical of the US. Some of the avenues (in the American sense), like St Vincent Street, achieve distinction, and some of the streets, like Buchanan Street, can be said to have elegance. There are townscapes which are, to their connoisseurs, as satisfying as any in Europe. What Glasgow does not have is that quality, possessed by parts of Edinburgh, of harmonious continuity. If Edinburgh has been inactive and complacent, content to preserve itself as an artefact in a museum, Glasgow has been sometimes careless of its own past; but it has variety, surprise and wonderful rewards for those who keep their eyes open. Even the cranes that stand above the empty berths along the river are powerful monuments to the dignity of an industrial tradition, and indeed some of them have acquired the status of listed buildings.

In these eight years I have been privileged to see the transformation of Glasgow. I arrived in a down-at-heel, demoralised town that seemed to be perched on the edge of the civilised world with every chance of falling into the abyss. On every hand were reminders of lost greatness or an evaporated sense of community. Now Glasgow is a proud and perky city with ambition. *The Economist* this year rather sourly said that Glasgow had 'hyped' its way back to prosperity. It is of course true that the change could not have been achieved without the efforts of the publicists. The Lord Provost of the day, Dr Michael Kelly, presided over these first efforts and the 'Glasgow's Miles Better' campaign was an instant success. What it meant was that Glasgow was miles better than it used to be, or people thought it was, but, in tune with the jealousies of Scottish life, folk in the capital thought it meant that Glasgow was miles better than Edinburgh; and so they coined the snide little riposte: Glasgow's miles *wetter*. No doubt it is; but Edinburgh is colder.

But the recovery of Glasgow is no figment of the imagination. It is the result of a very substantial investment by the public sector, flying rather in the face of Thatcherite doctrine. The Scottish Development Agency has been the midwife, but has allowed others, such as local authorities and the private sector, to take the credit. This has been a highly effective policy, in that it harnessed the goodwill of all parties; but it has had its political penalties, for the Government became concerned that it was deriving no political advantage from the efforts which it was largely funding. At the opening of the Garden Festival in 1988, we had the curious spectacle of the Lord Provost relegated to the second row of the official party, even though he is also the Lord Lieutenant and the Queen's representative, and yielding pride of place to a Secretary of State still smarting from his party's humiliation in Scotland in the General Election of the year before.

The physical refurbishment of Glasgow is a fact. There is now, of course, something of a new fashion, among girners and scribblers, to point out that it has 'done nothing' for the people in the housing schemes, for it is true that Glasgow has still got more than its due share of multiple deprivation and all the consequences that arise from it, and that those who live in the peripheral schemes – Scotland has an 'outer' rather than an 'inner' city problem – remain cast out into darkness. This criticism was more frequently heard as the Year of Culture, which Glasgow is celebrating in 1990, approached, and to it was added the comment that much of the culture being imported to the city would be elitist and of no value to ordinary folk. There is something patronising about this attitude, but it has undoubtedly created considerable political difficulties for those who had been organising 1990. It is, I think, misguided to adopt a pessimistic and miserable view of the enormous investment that has been made in Glasgow. It is true, of course, that the many new retail developments that have come our way do displace economic activity, rather than add to it. Yet it would be impossible to contemplate any kind of future for Glasgow without them. Competition among cities and regions will be the hallmark of Europe in the nineties. Without its exquisite Princes Square, without its concert hall, without the St Enoch Centre, Glasgow could simply not have kept afloat as a credible service and tourist centre, and if that means that some retailing must wither on the vine then it is a price that has to be accepted. The first bridge deprived a ferry crew of work, and nothing in the process of economic change can allow us to escape from that truth. Although change can be deferred, it cannot be denied, and Glasgow, with its memories of an industrial culture now more or less defunct, can testify to that.

Without the changes that have been wrought in the face and fabric of Glasgow, the city could have faced only continued decline. What is more questionable is whether the enormous public investment will produce a soundly based economic recovery. It is my clear impression that real progress has been made. Glasgow is no longer, to the outside world, a pariah among cities. Its university, which was strongly regional in character, is now beginning to attract students from all over the country. Executives and civil servants posted to Glasgow no longer regard it as Ultima Thule, though they still show a tendency to keep houses in the south against their eventual return. Tourists have begun to people the summer streets, even though they are a mere trickle when set beside the Edinburgh flood. And Glasgow people have begun to celebrate their new confidence as Europeans, and their new prosperity, by their enjoyment of dressing fashionably, even flashily, parading of an evening to the new generation of bars and restaurants that have supplanted the old howffs, and flying off at the drop of a sombrero to Spain.

Not everybody likes the new places, of course, and a friend of mine peers rather disgustedly round the pleasant, inn-like bar of Babbity Bowster's, in the Merchant City, and remarks that it looks a bit too clean. Like many a middle-class resident of a spick and span south-side villa, he has a nostalgic longing for the smoky bars of his youth, and prefers to patronise something that might be called a little more ethnic. It is in the Merchant City that we see the transformation at its best and its worst, depending on your point of view. To my mind the change is remarkably pleasing. The great beauty of old commercial buildings, offices and warehouses, constructed in an age when mercantile ambition was expressed in architectural flourish, has been revived by their conversion into flats. To others this process of gentrification, or 'yuppification', is an outrage since the people displaced from the Merchant City – itself a term which these critics denounce as affected and pretentious – cannot afford to live there any more. For my money the steady transformation of this area has to be rated as a triumph of planning, and its animation and liveliness, particularly at the weekend, as people flock to its shops and eateries, seems to refute the proposition that the ordinary folk are excluded from its joys. It is true that some of the conversions have been cheaply done by fly-by-nights; but others have enduring style. And it is true that housebreaking and opportunistic crimes are a curse of this area, as they are of many other parts of the UK, and that the impotence of the police to do anything about them is as clear here as it is elsewhere. Housebreaking is a crime that has become so routine in our cities that it now attracts little public notice, and I have some sympathy for those theorists who say that the reason for the high profile given by the authorities to the war against drugs arises from their inability to tackle problems nearer to home. When did we last hear a Government Minister promise a campaign against housebreaking?

Crime, sadly, does drag Glasgow down the European ratings in the periodic measurements that are made of the quality of life. Scotland does put more of its population in jail than any other country in civilised Europe. Yet it is not an illusion peddled by the hype-merchants that it is now as safe a city as its contemporaries. In my eight years in Glasgow I have had my share of the attention of criminals, with three housebreakings and a couple of vandalised cars (in the West End). Most were opportunistic crimes, obviously by youngsters, but one was by a burglar of the old school. He entered the house by the rone pipe. Once inside he worked his way down, meticulously emptying drawers and cupboards of anything

15

*The City
Chambers and
George Square,
1987.*

valuable (his haul was meagre – his competitors had already made off with the video); afterwards I felt a sneaking admiration for his cleanliness and his old-fashioned methods, just as I felt sympathy for the police in their impotence as they routinely and despairingly went through the motions of taking fingerprints and gathering evidence.

But I do not find Glasgow an unsafe or frightening city. I do treat it with respect, as I treat any other large city. I do not wander about Kelvinbridge at midnight if I can avoid it, for I remember that a colleague was attacked within an inch of his life there. There are parts of the city, as there are of Edinburgh, into which I never go. My Glasgow is particular to me, and there are large parts of it which never impinge on my life, and I am conscious of my privilege and good fortune. I walk with pleasure in the groves of the West End. I like the underground, the 'Clockwork Orange', but I avoid it when there's a game on at Ibrox. I am a habitué of the train to Edinburgh, but I avoid it when there's a game on in the capital involving a Glasgow team. I am an urban man and I know my jungle.

If I have dwelt on these aspects, it is because I too do not want to be accused of hype. But my Glasgow is a warm and friendly place, not at all frightening. Its love of enjoyment and of bright colours comes from various sources. One of them is its industrial and working-class tradition, which has produced the dandies who stroll the Merchant City of a Saturday night in their designer suits. Another is the Irish and Celtic strand in Glasgow, which has given us our taste for warm and vivid colours to brighten the sometimes dark skies. Another is the old Scottish tradition of hard work and a love of order. There is no greater antithesis in Scottish life than the neat surburban houses over the hill from housing schemes of anarchic disorder. Yet even that is changing as we try to correct the planning errors of the past.

Glasgow's greatest triumph as a city is that it has handled and absorbed social pressures that elsewhere have had disastrous results. I have referred to the safety vent of Old Firm rivalry. The other great vent is humour. Glasgow loves to laugh about the Old Firm; it loves to laugh at itself. But it does not like to be held in low opinion by others, and it thoroughly deserves its restored reputation. I have great pleasure in introducing the series of essays which try to convey its contemporary flavour.

WILLIAM HUNTER

The Glasgow Character

BECAUSE I WAS BROUGHT UP IN THE METROPOLITAN AREA OF PAISLEY, Glasgow sometimes seems small. Most square miles of it are much the same as each other square mile. It feels less like a city than a collection of townships. And there is the mystifying great divide of the Clyde. Glasgow people treat the stepping-stone stream of their river like an ocean wide. Although West-enders and South-siders like to insist they inhabit separate planets, they share another delusion that together they live at the centre of the universe. They tell a tale about two native sons lost in the Sahara for four days without food and without water for five. One wanderer shouts: 'Hey, do you know what day this is? It's Fair Friday.' Much gratified, his pal contemplates the molten sky: 'They've got a grand day for it,' he says. While every village imagines that its experience is universal, Glasgow people make a big belief of it, what they cannot take in is the wee notion that not everybody loves them.

Keelies (let's call them that name and get it over with) are suckers for their own propaganda. They have put it about so persuasively that they are only common old working chaps and their missuses that they have swallowed their own soft soap. In dire historical truth, Glasgow people have been as acquisitive as the Goths. In their territorial ambitions they were ungentle about whose homesteads they rolled over. Gorbals, Partick, Maryhill, Hillhead, Pollokshaws, and even Govan vanished into Glasgow's municipal maw. When the expanding frontier threatened to engulf Paisley (and Clydebank and Rutherglen), the natives there reached for their spears. The all-conquering keelies were stunned to be thrown back by teuchters – teuchters being a street word the keelies use not just for Highlanders but for everybody in the world who is not a keelie.

When the imperial advance of Glasgow's leaders was halted, they showed the cunning of all the Caesars. They sent in their tramcars to colonise the barbarians in the same way that the ancient Romans built roads. There was a war of words. Paisley still carries the wounds of Glasgow's imaginative abuse. So aptly concocted were some of the insults, they were accepted even by dictionaries. In the Scottish National Dictionary, like a boot in my ribs, resides the expression Paisley screwdriver, meaning a hammer. The libel is that Paisley craftsmen are clumsy and lazy. A Paisley knife is a corkscrew. Indelibly, Glasgow painted a picture of mean-spirited Paisley people always with a bottle opener on them, but never the price of a bottle.

Seeing off with their vocabulary anybody who stands in their way or gets in their light remains a joy and skill of Glasgow people. A wild poetry is their most effective fighting weapon and violence of tongue the greatest excess. The reputation for bloodier aggression is myth and tosh. For a former seaport populated by handy men and fearless women, Glasgow is a comparatively gentle city, which is to say it is not gentle at all. But it's a children's playground compared with the urban bullying that goes on even in Edinburgh or, perhaps, especially in Edinburgh. In forty years of knocking about Glasgow I have not seen a real fight, not one, although

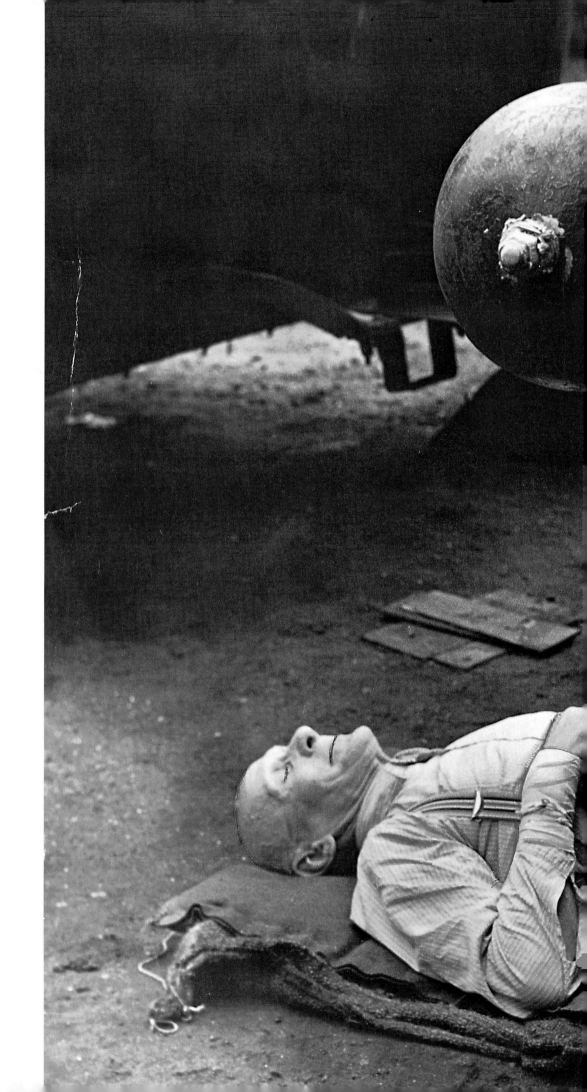

*Martin Breedis
then seventy,
alias Ivan Orloff,
balances a 220lb
weight on his
foot, 1954.*

*Tommy Morgan
on show.*

newspaper work sometimes leads me to dark corners because people who make headlines always seem to live up unlit stairs on top floors and to keep big dogs. Yet I have not experienced a real rammy, or not yet. I tell a lie, there was one. In a city-centre lounge bar two bears had a real go. One of them was a rough-handed clerk in a stockbroker's office and the other sold shirts in a haberdashery that specialised in military ties. Although the blue-chip hooligan finished the tourney looking as dead, because he raised his black hat to the barmaid when he was able to leave, on my card the result was a draw.

Glasgow's way with words, its patter, is hard stuff to analyse. Sometimes its humour receives the sociological explanation of being the bag of salt of keelie quickness mixed with Irish crack, Jewish sorrow and Highland romanticism. I wonder whether the roots are not economic. Humour does not spring from good health and robust optimism. It is more like a bright vapour that arises from a compost heap of deadly worry and desperation. Glasgow has been dying for all of this century. Only because its sinew and courage were needed in two wars did it not lie down.

Late in a bare tavern, a grey suit of a solicitor, a Partick Thistle supporter, was reading to bits the football acres of his Monday *Herald*. Because we knew each other slightly and because his team had scored a couple of wins in a row, I felt I should speak. But pub etiquette insisted we ignore each other because both of us should have been home hours earlier. When he'd folded his paper, he looked around and addressed nobody in particular. 'What Thistle need,' he said judiciously, 'is a decent run of losses.' Defeat he knew how to handle. When the world is benign and at your feet – when it's miles better – the vocabulary of the patter is short of things to say.

Because so much of the city's story has been harsh, getting a laugh out of it isn't easy. Glasgow's trick is to ignore the primary disasters and make a mountain of a secondary woe. Consider the story of two strangers who find out they were both at Dunkirk. One asks: 'When did you get away?' The answer comes: 'On the Thursday.' He is congratulated: 'You won a watch. It rained like buggery on the Friday.'

Cliff Hanley, writer and entertainer, treasures a Tommy Morgan story which the comic never told on the stage. In a Depression family the father is out of work, the children famished. 'Breid, breid,' they greet until the faither goes out for his dole money and to buy a loaf. Long hours pass. When he returns soaking wet, his countenance marked with grief, and with no bread, only much nagging by the wife gets an explanation. 'Have you no' seen the paper?' he explodes. 'The Prince of Wales has fell aff his horse.'

Glasgow lusts for action. Keelies are always looking for a new scene, even when they know it will unlikely be an improvement. The mood was entrapped for all time in a Bud Neill cartoon of a bauchle of a tram conductress. 'Quiet the day,' she says, 'I wish a cheeky wee man wid come on wi' six dugs, smoke doonsterrs, an' spit on the flerr.' There was the same restlessness in industry. Old Glasgow aye wanted to try something else. It gave up the tobacco trade when it didn't entirely need to (Bristol didn't give it up) and left most of textile manufacturing to Lancashire. The next wild decision was a too emotional embrace of the flighty, clarty jade of heavy engineering. Hindsight suggests that more concentration on carpets and precision instruments would have been wiser. Worse luck was how a chance at the craft of printing was let slip. An adventure with educated words was blighted by the failure of the Foulis brothers, Robert (who started out as a barber) and Andrew (who wanted to be a minister), eighteenth-century

Tommy Morgan.

*Flower-seller in
Glasgow's Union
Street, 1956.*

Herbert Byatt,
Glasgow street
musician, 1957.

printers to the old university. Their classical books remain a wonder, and they made an enlightened start to an academy of painting and sculpture. Glasgow could have had a brighter life with books than boats. Besides flourishing on a congenital addiction to words, a printing industry would have satisfied the traditional conviction of a working-class city that doing a full day's work means going home dirty. Being inky would have sufficed.

The failure of the Foulises has a compensation. With historical accuracy, Glasgow now can claim a renaissance. The present earnest obsession with the arts is truly a rebirth and not a first bite at the cultural cherry. A further connection to appeal to the gallus humour of the lieges is that, like the Foulis episode, artistic beanos usually end in splendid insolvency. Win or lose, in this city what matters is style. It was a bad time – twenty years ago, even as recently as ten years – when the streets had lost their swagger. In high places the voices of municipal leaders became whimpering girns. About the only recipe for recovery anybody could think of was the drafting of bowler-hat civil service jobs from Whitehall. Worse was the heavy air of defeat that lay on the plainstanes. The proprietorial stride of the citizens about the streets became shambling. They appeared to lose their heart even for jaywalking.

How life has returned to the pavements suggests an unquenchable source. In whatever next fine mess the city has got into, some spontaneous combustion has always revived its restlessness. Robert Southey, a visiting English poet, caught a whiff of inexhaustible warmth. In 1819 he said a mouthful in one pellucid sentence: 'A city like Glasgow is a hateful place for a stranger, unless he is reconciled to it by the comforts of hospitality and society.' In Glasgow, more than in most places, people are everything.

They are awkward. A medical officer of health of the old city corporation said he found the population full of folk who always wanted the toothpaste which the chemist didn't have. They are not easily impressed. In their own phrase, they do not readily burst oot in fairy lights. I was walking with a mate, a gnarled and wayward house painter, past the crystal place of the St Enoch shops, while he talked in long paragraphs about the causes and effects of the French Revolution. To the technological marvel of the new greenhouse (20,000 windows) he seemed not to give a glance. We had moved out of sight of the glass mountain before he thought it worth remarking: 'They'll need a right big shammy for that job.' At a football match of industrial efficiency but with no daft wee bits of artistic embroidery about it although Davie Cooper was then playing for the Rangers, a cry was wrung from the heart of one spectator: 'Aw, gie's a wee bit o' magic, Davie!' 'Aye, vanish!' responded his mate, a man heavily in tune with Glasgow's mixed mood of lively pessimism and its curt enthusiasm to deal from a new deck.

Alongside taking pride in being plain and proletarian sits a longing to be also perjink and proper. It is a part of the contrariness of the patter that a pub drinker in the throes of a stupendous bevvy will describe his bout as 'taking a wee refreshment'. A mother in the street to a snotty-nosed toddler will cry: 'Walk nice!' An inscrutable shop-window notice in a Bud Neill cartoon proclaims: 'Nice cheap messages.' Aspirations to gentility go along, no bother, with a determined working-class loyalty and closeness. In the crummiest tenements, prosperous families stayed on in wee palaces of houses to moan about a neighbour who put out a dirty washing.

In adjacent paragraphs of his memoirs, Sir James Lavery, the Irish-born artist, illustrated how the city is seamlessly made up of two cities. An advertisement in the *Herald* for an artist's model brought to his studio an unwashed, barefoot child, aged seven or eight, who described her job

BUD NEILL

" Nae clue, him. Here's us beltin' oot a chorus o'
" Silent Night " an' he chaps the door an' asks for
wur Hallowe'en . . . "

Bud Neill.

*An interior view
of a streamlined
Glasgow tram.*

Argyle Street,
1959.

Fiddler in
Sauchiehall
Street, 1961.

Street characters.

'Fares, please' on
the route to
Auchenshuggle,
1962.

experience with a stained-glass painter. As she put it: 'Ah was posing for an angel, and he gave me saxpence an 'oor in ma claes and ninepence in ma skin.' Later, when Lavery was painting the garden scene from Faust, he hired a genteel miss with whom Faust got familiar in the greenhouse they used for a changing-room. Missie told her friends: 'I would not have went if I had knew.' A hidden point of Lavery's recollections is that the two models could have been the same girl at different ages. For this is one tough town in which to have social pretensions. A lawyer and a brickie's labourer will stay mates because they grew up in the same street and continue to meet without any sense of being unequal, even on the part of the lawyer.

While one legacy of an industrial past is that everybody keeps shouting as if trying to be heard above the noise of heavy machinery, another is that under the plain, hard surface of the bellowing there bubbles much sweet sentimentality. It surfaces at rare times of frank emotion. On the south side of sobriety it seldom finds expression in words.

At my one visit to old-time Wembley, Scotland gave a 3–2 doing to the Saxons, who happened to be calling themselves world champions at the time. After taking a refreshment, I fell on to the top bunk of a train sleeper from Euston. At wakey-wakey time the mouth felt like the inside of Jim Baxter's stockings. Silently over the rim of the bed appeared a bottle of Irn Bru. With my provident companion from downstairs, who turned out to be a van driver and a Clyde supporter, there was a happy hour of living the triumph all over again, while we took our mornings of his Bru and what we could find in our half-bottles.

The nearer the train got to Glasgow, the more the early Sunday hours promised to be the start of another great day. Perfect happiness was being further improved with golden sunshine from an operatic blue sky. At the sight of the first corporation bus – looking lost and shy the way they all do from a train as if not sure of the way back to town – the wee man tidied his appearance with wetted fingers and made a check of the presents he had for his grandchildren. He readied away the remains of our picnic. He reckoned he still had left the price of his bus fare home to Bridgeton. Going over the river bridge, he remarked that that would be the wife getting up and putting the frying pan on. He said he could smell the square sausages and the black pudding already. Outside the station we shook hands goodbye.

Walking away round the camera shop corner, he paused and raised his arms above his head, his carrier bag dangling from a wrist, and did a wee jig to himself. His bantam figure embodied bliss. There was a man so adept at living his life that for a foreseen emergency he knew a way to keep by him a bottle of his favourite ginger for two nights and a day. He was a survivor. His little dance was when I began to see what it is to belong to Glasgow and for it to belong to you. Man and place were an exact fit. He was home where there is no better place.

Doc Holliday, alias John Kerley, takes a stroll in Buchanan Street during the Glasgow Busking Festival.

Tanks at the
Cattle market,
Glasgow Strike,
1919.

MURRAY RITCHIE

The Political Culture in Glasgow

SOME MIGHT SAY THAT GLASGOW'S POLITICAL CULTURE IS SO uncomplicated that it can be summed up in three words in one second: one-party state. It is an awfully tempting conclusion, but wrong. The simple arithmetic of Labour's heavy domination of parliamentary and municipal representation is misleading. Ever since the smell of revolution pervaded Europe after 1917 – and became particularly pungent on Clydeside – Glasgow's political life has differed in its reality from the perception of those looking in from the outside. Paradoxes are the stuff of Glasgow politics. The place has spent decades threatening politically to be something it is not and never was. Glasgow looks like a hard-nosed soviet but in its heart it is more of a pink softie. For revolutionary, read radical, with reservations.

In the final decade of the twentieth century Glasgow is the inheritor of a system of electoral representation which grievously distorts the truth about the political sympathy of Glaswegians. The arithmetic shows, for example, that sixty of the district council's sixty-six members are Labour and that the Tories can muster only four councillors and the nationalists none. That bears little relation to the share of votes cast in municipal elections. But the lie becomes even more blatant when parliamentary representation is examined. Even before the third Thatcher General Election victory Glasgow was a Tory-free zone. Only Roy Jenkins of the SDP in Hillhead spoiled the symmetry of Labour's sweep through the city's eleven parliamentary seats and when he was toppled by George Galloway in 1987 Labour's domination became complete. Jim Sillars of the Scottish National Party broke the pattern again in a famous by-election in late 1988 but he, too, has just as high a profile as a socialist than as a nationalist.

Thus Glasgow is perceived to be a city which rejects anti-socialist political candidates as a matter of routine although the share of votes cast in elections tells another story. This electoral distortion spills over into other parts of Strathclyde whose regional council has its headquarters in the city centre. Strathclyde has 103 regional councillors of whom eighty-seven are Labour but such an imbalance in no way accurately reflects the electoral sympathy of the region in which Glasgow is by far the largest single electoral block. Thus Glasgow's reputation as a Scottish soviet is reinforced.

Forces other than the electoral system have led to this ridiculous misrepresentation. The most significant is the easiest to explain. Back in the early seventies when Mr Gordon Campbell was the Scottish Secretary of State in Mr Edward Heath's Cabinet, the Scottish Tory leadership suffered a fateful and near fatal collapse of the will to survive in municipal politics. When the Wheatley Commission produced its proposals for the reform of local government the Scottish Office lost no time in meddling with them. The interference was so extensive that after the Local Government (Scotland) Act 1973 had become effective and the regional and district council system, introduced in May 1975, was firmly in place Lord Wheatley was moved to make a public disclaimer of responsibility for the final result. In effect, the Tories in Scotland committed electoral suicide. In Strathclyde, for example,

The Red Flag in front of the City Chambers, George Square, 1919.

The juvenile
representatives in
the Rent Strike,
1915.

political control over half of the population of Scotland was handed to Labour in perpetuity. Majorities were so large as to be immovable even in the wildest dreams of the scuttled Tories. On Glasgow district council the same applied to a slightly lesser extent but in restructured Glasgow politics the memory of a long succession of anti-socialist administrations in the City Chambers was fresh. As recently as the late seventies Labour had been fended off when the SNP held the balance of power and sided with a Conservative administration in George Square. It was only after 1975 that the Scottish Tories began to recognise the awfulness of their mistake: it was no less than a wilful act of self-destruction, one from which they have never recovered and probably never will until the time comes again for another reform of Scottish local government. For the near total removal of Conservative voices from Glasgow's municipal affairs has been reflected throughout Scotland where at the time of writing the Tories control only three of the country's fifty-three district councils. They control not one of the nine Scottish regional authorities. Glasgow's rejection of Conservatism in the Thatcher mould has had reverberations in parliamentary representation throughout Scotland where only ten Tory MPs survive and where the confident expectation around the country is that even fewer will be returned to Westminster at the next General Election. In that sense Glasgow's political bent seems to have been influential throughout the country. At present Scotland's other cities, Edinburgh, Aberdeen and Dundee, are also Labour-controlled. With each successive round of council elections the consequences of botched local government reform grow even more appalling for the Tories.

So, in assessing the contemporary political culture of Glasgow we must first recognise the artificial face which Glasgow (and other Scottish cities and towns) puts on because of this singular act of Conservative administrative folly; and we are entitled to wonder at the enormity of the political misjudgment which helped to give Glasgow its reputation, however undeserved, for socialist commitment, a commitment so fervent that it could scarcely have been envisaged even by the fabled Red Clydesiders who first provided the city with its paradoxical politics all those decades ago. Glasgow is Labour, of that there is no question, but for seventy years or so it has never threatened revolution. Far from it. As we shall see, the years since the First World War have seen Labour consolidate its role in Glasgow politics to the point that it has become the party of the political Establishment, careful, conservative, often reactionary and increasingly bureaucratic.

Until the closing years of the last century Glasgow was Liberal until the Irish Question began to colour British politics. With a large proportion of its population being Irish, Glasgow began to reflect the Liberals' division on that issue. The curse of sectarianism which was evident then has stayed with Glaswegians ever since and political party managers will still privately admit that it is a factor, although much less critical, today in the city's political culture. It was not until the seventies that Conservatives in municipal elections called themselves Conservatives. Until then they had been Unionists, or at least members of the Unionist Party, standing as Progressives. (Elsewhere in Scotland Conservatives often presented themselves as Moderates and in some of the regions they still stand today as Independents despite being card-carrying Tories.) But as Unionists they spent years successfully exploiting the Protestantism of the Glaswegian majority. For this reason the substantial Catholic vote came easily to Labour in the west of Scotland. Catholic clergy urged their congregations to reject Unionism with its anti-Irish overtones and Labour emerged after the Liberal collapse as the principal opposition to Unionism/Conservatism. Nowadays

John McLean, 1919.

James Maxton.

the Orange/Green division is never exploited in public by politicians and there seems little doubt that in so far as it exists at all it is confined to the far margins although the Tories will point out, in private, that most Glasgow Labour councillors are Catholic. Looked at another way, it is also fair to dismiss that as insignificant. Most Glasgow Catholics, after all, are Labour and it would be surprising if their councillors were otherwise. Religious groupings did, undeniably, show up strongly in Labour's early days and played an important part in vote-winning by Unionists in what was and still is an overwhelmingly working-class city. In modern Glasgow working-class Tories are a rarity. Indeed a principal reason for Labour's recent electoral successes is the absence in Glasgow of a significant middle class. Conservative middle-class voters long ago decamped to the suburbs of Bearsden and Milngavie, Newton Mearns, Bishopbriggs and elsewhere and from these fringe redoubts they successfully fought off inclusion in Glasgow when the boundaries were being redrawn after the Wheatley Commission's report. Only now, after more than a decade of inner-city redevelopment, are they beginning to return to the city centre.

It was the politics of housing, or the lack of it, which helped to unite Glasgow's working class and it is housing which remains the single most important working-class issue in the city today. Housing has permeated all political thinking in Glasgow for all of this century when slum clearance and its chaotic results have become an enduring part of Glasgow political life. In the last years of the nineteenth century, when Labour began winning seats on Glasgow Town Council, housing in the city was in crisis. The slums were at bursting point, life had become intolerable for tens of thousands of poor people. By the time Britain was fighting the Great War the passions raised by sub-standard housing had become almost uncontainable. People took to the streets in support of rent strikes. On the walls of the People's Palace museum in Glasgow Green and in the file room of the *Glasgow Herald* the pictorial record is compelling even today. Families carrying placards protested: 'My father is fighting in France. We are fighting the Hun at home' – the Hun being private Glasgow landlords. 'We are fighting the Prussians of Partick,' said one placard whose bearer demanded municipal housing. In addition to the widespread unrest caused by poor housing Glasgow also had to endure a series of strikes at the very time the Second City of the Empire was powering British industry and supporting the war effort. This, too, helped to unite impoverished working-class voters. Events moved to a dramatic climax in the second year of the Great War when tanks were sent into George Square and the Red Flag flew to popular acclaim. At that point the Russian revolution was still reverberating throughout Europe and the British authorities were alarmed that revolution was not far off at home. Glasgow at that point began to gain its reputation for being a socialist citadel in the centre of the Red Clydeside. That phrase, Red Clydeside, has remained part of the political vocabulary of Glasgow's socialist romantics. In truth the possibility of the revolution taking place was fleeting. The conventional view of those events today is revisionist: that while those famous protests served the useful purpose of concentrating the Establishment mind they never seriously threatened full-scale bloody insurrection with the purpose of turning Scotland into a socialist republic. The authorities did feel sufficiently discomfited to take local regiments off the street and confine them to barracks in Maryhill lest their sympathies led them to join in the popular demonstrations of protest. Soldiers from England faced the crowds in George Square. But Red Clydeside is otherwise mythology, a stirring notion sustained and promoted by idealists who desperately wished the revolution had indeed come about at that time and who regret that it never did.

Events in that early part of the century produced some fine Glasgow politicians and socialist activists whose names are now part of the city's folklore, among them Jimmy Maxton, John Wheatley, John Maclean and Emmanuel Shinwell who lived to celebrate his hundredth birthday and to observe the coming of Thatcherism. A few years before his death he was asked by Ian Imrie of the *Glasgow Herald* to talk about Red Clydeside. Shinwell was happy to reminisce about his activities in those days but when the phrase Red Clydeside came into the conversation, he replied: 'There was never any such thing.'

In the twenties Labour made the breakthrough when it gained a solid majority of Glasgow parliamentary seats, having campaigned hard on the housing issue and called for rent controls which were imposed during the Great War to be maintained. Meanwhile, outside the Commons, John Maclean was becoming a socialist folk hero of the streets of Glasgow, preaching revolution in Scotland in support of the world's first workers' state in Russia. For his trouble he went to jail where he was force-fed, and he died broken and defeated. Maclean is celebrated today as the martyr who 'forged the Scottish link in the golden chain of world socialism' but he achieved almost nothing except the reverence of latter-day romantics.

Since inheriting a large share of Glasgow's and Scotland's political sympathy back in the early years of this century Labour has been careful to avoid falling into the Home Rule trap which killed the early Liberals. For Labour the Irish question has never quite disappeared and is still potentially divisive. In Glasgow, Ireland has meant sectarianism and sectarianism has always threatened to split the growing Labour vote. It was Labour in Glasgow which encouraged the policy of the right to separate schooling for Roman Catholics so that the party could be shown worthy of Catholic working-class support. Perhaps by way of unconscious repayment it has traditionally been reticent about the Irish question and been careful to avoid it wherever possible. As a direct consequence Labour has become in its own way strongly unionist, a policy which landed it in trouble in the seventies with its reluctance to embrace even limited devolution in Scotland. As Scottish public opinion swung behind the idea of limited Home Rule in the early seventies and the Labour leadership in London saw the need to rethink its centralist policies, the Scottish Labour conference remained stoically against constitutional change. Labour suffered the humiliation of being told by London to hold another conference (in Glasgow) and this time to change its collective mind and make preparations for a Scottish Assembly. Mr Willie Ross, long serving Scottish Secretary and lifelong Harold Wilson loyalist, who was known to have deep suspicions about the very idea of decentralisation, put on a brave face when he went on television and was asked for his reaction to the inevitable and embarrassing about-turn. 'I have always been a devolutionist,' Mr Ross remarked with a straight face.

And so, while the Irish Question of long ago still produces faint echoes in Labour's unionist and constitutional nervousness today, the net result has been helpful to Glasgow. It is to the eternal credit of Glasgow, separate schools and all, and to the city's politicians from all parties, that the sectarianism which undoubtedly still exists has never been permitted to flare in response to the past twenty years of conflict across the Irish Sea. One of these faint echoes was heard last year in Hillhead where Mr George Galloway was in trouble with his constituency executive over a series of highly publicised misdemeanours. When he decided to travel to

An overturned bus being righted during the General Strike, 1926.

Rents protest march, 1951.

Dublin to join a march of Sinn Fein supporters half his executive resigned in protest and denounced his integrity. They had been prepared to suffer their MP's high-living on expenses from a charity and his confessions of sexual adventures but going to Dublin, publicly to support Irish republicanism was too much.

In present-day Glasgow Labour has become accustomed to being the natural party of power. It is one of the urban rocks on which Labour throughout Britain wants to build the foundation for its next government. It is the place which Harold Wilson and Jim Callaghan used as the starting point for General Election campaigns. Wilson in particular always found himself at home in the city and used his visits to Glasgow to make long policy speeches, some of which were tortuously dull and which sympathetic Glasgow audiences had to endure so that the erstwhile Prime Minister could say at some future occasion: 'I made the point in my Glasgow speech.' While Glasgow has stayed loyal to Labour during its ten years of infighting and national electoral defeat the party has achieved little in power in the City Chambers. Even the residual powers which the district council inherited after reorganisation have been limited by Thatcherism and the new philosophy that local government should be merely a cypher for centralist authority. Only housing – as ever – remains in the domain of Glasgow district council and even that, the holiest of Labour cows in the municipal byre, will soon be taken from it. For Labour that is a huge threat. Glasgow politics is so bound up in housing that even Labour's survival cannot be guaranteed in an era when the council is no longer a benevolent landlord to more than half of the city's electors. The gradual loss of housing control will eventually shake Labour from its easy life in the City Chambers and the parliamentary divisions. Already the SNP has proved in Govan (twice) that it can be successful by showing itself to be more anti-Tory than the national Opposition. The Conservatives themselves are being reorganised, although probably in the wrong direction for Glaswegian electoral tastes. Glasgow has never been strongly Tory, preferring in anti-Labour phases to support watered down Toryism (Moderates, Independents, Progressives) but its in-built radicalism has no time for the Toryism of Margaret Thatcher. In a curious way Glasgow's electors are conservative. Today's Labour council is filled with 'safe' Labour councillors. In Glasgow you will not find much successful activity by, for example, Militant Tendency, whose principal organiser recently gave up the unequal struggle for revolution. He became a journalist. You will not find the heirs of Marx and Lenin in the marbled corridors of the City Chambers where the green-tailed flunkies serve tea from silver platters to the people's champions who drive around in the municipal Roller.

One of these days the British Tories will lose a General Election and a new Government of whatever complexion will change the Constitution. Glasgow and Scotland as a whole will have a new system of Government, central and local, probably with a reformed electoral system. When that happens Labour must again learn to live in the real political world and not the cushioned world of mythology, complacency and self-deception which is Glasgow's lot now.

*Margaret
Thatcher surveys
the Glasgow
Garden Festival,
1988.*

*Jim Sillars and
actor Iain McColl
campaigning for
the SNP at
Govan, 1988.*

Harold Wilson MP speaks at Queen's Park, 1959.

No go situation as the Civic Rolls Royce resists attempts by mechanics to re-start, 1985.

Govan
shipbuilders,
1987.

ALF YOUNG

Glasgow's Economy and Industry

THERE ARE TWO CONTRASTING DIAGNOSES OF THE INDUSTRIAL AND commercial health of Glasgow in the 1990s which seem to me equally pernicious. The first draws its sombre conclusions from a debilitating nostalgia for times past when the city made far, far more things than it does today.

Those who look back with the deepest yearning probably see the City of Culture accolade as a tinpot decoration, a tarnished shadow of the days when Glasgow was Second City of the Empire, a manufacturing and commercial powerhouse on the Clyde. I, too, can walk round that room in the Museum of Transport and feel my heart ache, measuring case after case of hand-crafted Clyde-built ship models against the silent dereliction that grips much of the river today. The icons for our angst are straw railway engines hung from dockside cranes and paper boats bobbing on an unbustled river.

Those of us who number ourselves the first generation in our families to turn our backs on the tools and don white collars, are often the biggest culprits. And there are plenty of us. 'What will become of us,' we cry, 'if we don't make things anymore?' And, as we write our stories, audit another set of accounts, teach, advise, administer, sell, distribute, advertise or consult, we secretly worry about how much longer we can survive by taking in each other's washing.

Doubtless the same concerns troubled earlier generations of Glaswegians as they watched, helpless, while that Second City reputation began to crumble: when the great chimney of the St Rollox chemical works was dynamited in 1923 . . . the last railway engine built in Springburn was shipped off to some corner of the Empire where it still steams along to this day . . . or Dixon's Blazes – the blast furnaces of the Govan Iron Company – no longer glowed in the south-side sky. The loss of manufacturing capacity – and the jobs and skills which go with it – is a tragedy when that capacity still has productive life left in it, but is sacrificed to some politically induced recession.

However there are deeper tides in the industrial evolution of any community – the decline of Glasgow's nineteenth-century cotton mills drowned out by the growing clang of metal-bashing, for example – when resistance is futile. Pride in past achievement has its honourable place. But at these times the only constructive course is to confine nostalgia to the bookshelf, museum room or trade union banner, close a door on what went before and concentrate on fresh opportunities ahead. Glasgow, throughout the 1980s, has been facing up, slowly and painfully, to just such a fundamental transition. However, in the process, we run the risk of arriving, prematurely, at a second, equally pernicious conclusion.

It is that, given a few licks of PR gloss, some city centre sandblasting and a festival or two, Glasgow emerges in its new party frock, a fully fledged, post-industrial phonomenon. A city whose economic future is assured, without making a single damned thing if it doesn't want to.

*View of the Clyde
from a crane in
John Brown's
shipyard, 1959.*

*Govan
Shipbuilders,
1976.*

*River Clyde
looking west
from Finnieston
Ferry.*

*Aerial view of
Glasgow Garden
Festival, 1988.*

It isn't that simple, of course. The glitz may attract more tourists. The new-found self-confidence may delude Glaswegians with a job into thinking that all the problems have been cracked, that their city truly is the Barcelona of the North, marketing its 'buzz' to the footloose searching out the latest fashion in urban landscapes. But the new frock has a grubby hem, stained by the reality of that seventeen percent or so of its citizens who are still out of work. Reading the latest civic brochure designed to attract new investment to the city, you'd never guess that, as it was being produced, complete with tributes from everyone from the Queen to a clutch of incoming businessmen, twenty-three percent of Glasgow men . . . yes, nearly one in four . . . were still without a job. No wonder the head of establishment from the Ministry of Defence could say, in his contribution, 'We have had absolutely no difficulty in recruiting very good quality staff. In fact we are almost embarrassed with riches.'

In the age of the sound bite and the photo-opportunity, such uncomfortable realities are stage-managed into the shadows by PR machines. The gloss is not unique to Glasgow. Every city seeking an alternative economic future – from Pittsburg to Hamburg, from Newcastle to Lille – is painting itself in the same fresh, bright, videodrome colours. But what, in Glasgow's case, lies beneath the gloss?

Geography hasn't done the city any favours in preparing it for the end of 1992 when major barriers to free trade within the European Community are due to come down. The Clyde lies on the wrong side of the country to exploit the single market by sea. The river's Port Authority is more dependent on property deals involving derelict docks these days than revenue from sparse river traffic.

Glasgow lies, too, on the fragile periphery of that market of 320 million people. Its road, rail and air links with where the real action is – the Ruhr, Paris, Milan triangle – are, as yet, grossly inadequate. Viewed from George Square, mainland Europe seen through the Channel Tunnel is still akin to surveying the honeypot through the wrong end of a telescope.

Within Scotland, Glasgow's traditional dominance in manufacturing industry has long since been toppled. The two main growth sectors in manufacturing in the seventies and eighties – the downstream support industries feeding offshore oil exploration and electronics – have largely passed the city by. They found oil under the North Sea, leaving Glasgow, again stranded on the other side of the country, to scramble for a few crumbs of spin-off business.

The incoming American and Japanese companies, who dominate electronics, had no interest in brownfield city sites haunted by the ghosts of past industrial failure. Such inward investors opted instead for the manicured campuses of Scotland's five new towns, or, if they gauged Locate in Scotland's hunger acute enough, demanded that their up-market sheds be set down in the kind of sylvan parkland settings that were previously the preserve of landed gentry.

Glasgow's overspill – often the young and ambitious – followed the work. Yet by 1984, Strathclyde Region, which includes Glasgow and three of these new towns, had a smaller proportion of its working population in manufacturing (25.9 per cent) than either Fife (30 per cent) or Borders (35.8 per cent).

Some of the city's older manufacturing industries have survived, albeit in truncated form. There is still shipbuilding on the upper reaches of the Clyde, which is more than you can say for Sunderland and the Wear. Glasgow's engineering tradition persists, turning out everything from pumps and lorry axles to periscopes and aero-engine parts. The rag trade and the whisky blenders, printers and food processors, are all prominent in the depleted ranks of Glaswegians who still make things.

They still make things in factories which are, in scale, pale shadows of the Beardmores or Singers of yesteryear. They make things within communities which are no longer in awe of tradesmen. And they make things for owners who are more likely to be headquartered in London, mainland Europe or North America than in West Regent or West George Street. The old industrial dynasties which employed countless thousands in past generations and shaped so much of the commercial life of the Glasgow area over two centuries, the families whose wealth brought the city much of its rich Victorian architectural legacy and stimulated the early growth of the Scottish financial services sector, have largely faded from the scene. Tennant, Colville, Coats, Stephen, Collins, Weir, Yarrow, Fraser and a few dozens more. . . . Some progressed from machine shop to banking parlour. Some lost out to nationalisation. Some fell out among themselves. Some came to the end of the family line. Collectively their influence is greatly diminished and whether we mourn or applaud its passing, for Glasgow their going poses one crucial question. Who or what will replace the dynamic these dynasties once helped generate?

The mantle can hardly fall on the Kvaerners of this world, the new Norwegian owners of Govan Shipbuilders. They are here (and there is still merchant shipbuilding on the Clyde rather than the Wear) because they preferred Govan's facilities to the Sunderland yards of North East Shipbuilders.

Younger home-bred industrial and business dynasties run from Glasgow are as rare as cranes on the riverbanks these days. Hence Sir Norman Macfarlane's ubiquitous presence. Faced with the choice of building their business into a stock-market force themselves or selling out, after a decade say, to a more remote purchaser, west of Scotland entrepreneurs are prone to take the money and run.

At a visible level, Glasgow's major businesses are increasingly externally controlled. Six years ago, Glasgow Action set out to cement existing private/public partnerships in the city by persuading businesses elsewhere, particularly in the congested south-east of England, to relocate their headquarters on Clydeside. But the task of weaning British businessmen away from the London nexus and the Shuttle mentality has proved infinitely harder than anyone realised.

Major office developments in the city, first touted around as ideal locations for the incomers, have welcomed some relocated civil service departments and a few frontier-busting service industries from elsewhere but, far more commonly, have been let to local businesses and existing branch offices trading up-market. Glasgow's lawyers and accountants have led the way, swopping the bare lino and antique telephone exchange for deep-pile carpets, computer networks and real art on the walls. It's a welcome transition but its potential for keeping the local office property market on the boil is certainly finite. Yet new and refurbished office developments, improved hotel and leisure facilities and a series of major retail shopping malls are the most tangible landmarks of Glasgow's current economic renaissance.

If the office property boom looks distinctly finite, the city's retail revolution – lured by the belief that the Glasgow of the eighties was woefully undershopped and fired by the expectation that each successive development could relieve the citizens of some of their higher-than-average (given lower

*The Forge
Shopping Centre,
Parkhead, 1989.*

*George Wyllie's
straw locomotive
dangling,
Mayfest 1987.*

*The Wyllie
'Paper Boat'
floating on the
Clyde after its
launch, 1989.*

*The Forum Hotel
with lights
outside the North
Rotunda
Restaurant in the
foreground,
1989.*

The Stock Exchange, 1983.

property costs) disposable income – looks equally vulnerable. Recession on Argyle Street would quickly, and very publicly, wipe a lot of the gloss off Glasgow's current conceit of itself.

Who else, then, will sustain us in Glasgow's post-industrial old age? In many British cities the financial services industry is one of the main creators of new jobs. Glasgow still boasts its own stock exchange unit – though trading floors have given way to computer screens – but, with honourable exceptions, Glasgow's money movers do not have the collective clout of Edinburgh's. Scotland's capital is struggling, in turn, to avoid being overtaken by the likes of Manchester. And all, inevitably, are dwarfed by the sheer scale of the City of London.

If Glasgow has any local business heroes left, they are probably that low-profile assortment of restaurant and wine bar owners, property developers, niche retailers, sports and arts impresarios, small builders and straight barrow boys, for whom the current love affair with Glasgow is an opportunity to turn another shilling or two. I admire their boundless optimism and their reserve when it comes to displaying the fruits of their labours. Newcastle, not Glasgow, they tell me, is the Porsche capital of the UK. I know big chunks of Glasgow's legal and accountancy professions are now dependent on their efforts to continue earning the kind of fat crusts they are used to. What worries me is the bewildering speed with which these remaining heroes flit across Glasgow's commercial destiny.

It took nearly 170 years for the publishing business built by that first William Collins to succumb to the tentacles of Rupert Murdoch's worldwide media empire. It took just as long for the Tennant family to amass a fortune making bleach in the biggest chemical works in Europe, at St Rollox, and end up as copy for the gossip columns from the beaches of Mustique. These days in Glasgow, the fortunes made are of more modest proportions. And they seem to be created and squandered, in some cases, faster than you can say 'City of Culture'. Receivers with fewer big factory closures on their hands, chase mounting personal insolvencies in the leisure sector, where today's hot spot can change hands four or five times in its first couple of years before becoming tomorrow's boarded-up redevelopment opportunity.

Perhaps we all have to learn to live with life permanently running in fast-forward mode. But that renders Glasgow's commercial future infinitely more fragile. If fashion becomes the main arbiter of where we will all be in ten years time, we had better enjoy our time in the sun. A decade on, more of us may have experience of being Glaswegian and unemployed.

STEWART LAMONT

Religion in the City

THE JEWEL IN GLASGOW'S ECCLESIASTICAL CROWN IS THE CATHEDRAL. Not only is it the finest surviving and complete example of Scotland's ecclesiastical buildings, it is the foundation stone of the city itself. Shrouded in the swirling of Celtic and Pictish mists in the year 601 AD, it received the body of St Mungo or Kentigern who founded a 'stately church' on its site. He has been described as the 'cuckoo in the nest' of Celtic saints, owing to his habit of swallowing their legends which were then attributed to him. Other than Pictish lineage and a spell in Wales, little is known about him or the working of the monastery he left on the banks of the Molendinar.

Five hundred years elapsed before the see of Glasgow awakened to the sound of stonemasons' hammers and the erection of the present building in 1136 by John Achaius, bishop of Glasgow.

Then in 1484, Robert Blackadder, a liberal prelate who spent vast sums on his diocese, was repaid with its elevation to an archbishopric. He played a role in arranging the marriage of James IV to Henry VIII's daughter which led to the Union of the Crowns in the person of James VI and I. But the Reformation in 1560 saw the twilight of the god-like prelates who had presided over the medieval churches like mini-popes. Grabbing the gold and silver and the books of the archdiocese, Archbishop James Beaton high-tailed it for France. Thus began the tribal war between Protestants and Catholics which has dominated the religious history of Glasgow and has at times made Rangers–Celtic encounters look like football games.

To begin with the Kirk had the field to itself. Attempts by the anglified Charles I to subdue it through the introduction of episcopacy got short shrift from the Glasgow General Assembly of 1638. Although the King got wind of their intentions and dissolved the Assembly, they still went ahead and voted out his bishops. That same dissenter spirit made the West a happy hunting ground for Covenanters in the seventeenth century and showed itself in 1689 when Glasgow levied and armed a whole battalion in support of William of Orange within a day. And a century later, in 1779 when the granting of civil liberties to Roman Catholics was under discussion in Parliament, eighty-five societies numbering over 12,000 persons were formed in Glasgow – over a quarter of the population.

However, during the seventeenth and eighteenth centuries, Glasgow grew very slowly. Until 1600 it had consisted of only one parish. The Barony congregation formed in 1595 met in the undercroft of the Cathedral, a dismally unsuitable place in which to preach. Life was generally fairly dismal since the puritanical morals were reinforced under the Calvinist system. The kirk session had powers to compel moral offenders to appear before them. There were plenty of laws against sabbath-breaking but the most common offences were sexual and there must have been no need for the *News of the World* in the seventeenth century when you could watch sinners squirm on the cutty stool in front of the congregation, their cheeks turning as scarlet as their sins. Failure to appear to swallow your medicine was punishable with severe civil penalties. In 1652 the kirk session of Glasgow actually

*Glasgow
Cathedral, a view
down Wishart
Street from
Alexandra
Parade, 1962.*

paid 'spies' to report on lapses among the congregation. The parish was small, and so were the minds.

But if it was small it was beautiful. Daniel Defoe could write of it in 1707, 'It is a large stately and well built city standing on a plain in a manner four square and the five principal streets are the fairest for breadth and the finest built I have ever seen in one city together . . . in a word 'tis one of the cleanliest, most beautiful and best built cities in Great Britain.' Prior to the industrial revolution Glasgow still was distinct and different in its demography. In 1773 it had five times less gentry than Edinburgh. Tradesmen and merchants ruled the roost.

Then came the deluge. Between 1801 and 1831 Glasgow's population grew from 77,000 to 202,000. The towns grew rich and acted as magnets for the rural population. By 1840 there were 47,318 sittings in the established Kirk and 34,852 among the other Protestants, mostly United Secession churches, and many were unlet. There were eighty-five places of worship in Glasgow in 1840; of which forty belonged to the Kirk, thirty-nine to the dissenters, four to Episcopalians and two to the Roman Catholics.

The latter had completed a chapel in 1816 with 2,200 sittings in Great Clyde Street at a cost of £14,000 which made it the most expensive and the grandest of the non-established Christian churches. It was nearly not built. Guards had to be posted each night to prevent zealous Prots from knocking down the previous day's work. And that was before the Irish influx began in earnest.

Not all Protestant zeal was directed towards Catholics. The unfortunate Rev William Ritchie of St Andrew's near Glasgow Cross in 1807 fell foul of the Town Clerk when he introduced an organ (the first in Scotland in a parish kirk) with the consent of his congregation. Notwithstanding this, the Lord Provost persuaded the Presbytery that this was illegal and out it came. When Mr Ritchie moved to Edinburgh the press carried a cartoon of him with a barrel organ on his back playing, 'We'll gang nae mair tae yon toun'.

It is wrong to think of the nineteenth century as a glorious period of religious activity. The 1843 church/state conflict known as the Disruption had the effect of a civil war, sapping the churches' energies while a vast empire of poverty and social decay grew up unchecked. In some parts of Glasgow in 1871, four-fifths of the people had no church connection and in the East End there was one church for every 5,800. Meanwhile the rival Kirks raced each other into the suburbs, building rival places of worship on opposite corners of the street. In 1876 Glasgow Free Church Presbytery did not regard a church as necessary in Pollokshields but could not resist the pressure of wealthy laymen who wanted it there and were willing to sell a 'Free Kirk' in a poor district to help pay for it. The Gorbals was by 1830 already akin to the black hole of Calcutta, yet the Kirk managers there could find time to ask the Court of Session to determine which of two beadles appointed by them was rightful 'bethral' (as he was called). In a judgement of Solomon, the minister Dr James McLean dispensed with both and carried the Bible under his oxter into the tub himself.

In the 1870s there were three rivals – the Church of Scotland, the Free Church and the United Presbyterian (formerly Secession) Church. All were roughly similar in outlook, worship and doctrine and, with the abolition of patronage in 1874, had not much to quarrel about (or so you might imagine). But it was not until 1900 that the UP and the Free Churches united to form the United Free Church which then rejoined the Church of Scotland in 1929. In Glasgow it created the biggest Presbytery in the world since all that fission

Pastor Jack Glass, minister of the Zion Sovereign Grace Baptist Church, 1969.

and fusion had created a plethora of churches which belonged to the same denomination. As decline in church attendance plummeted in the twentieth century they closed, united, sold up and dissolved into the landscape.

In the sixties the M8 cut a swathe through the city and the world's biggest Presbytery was fortunate to have as its Presbytery Clerk, a qualified lawyer, the Rev Andrew Herron, who wheeled and bulldozed his way through the deals that would give the Kirk compensation for demolition of churches and planning permission to build new churches for old in the outer housing estates. His personal history of the parishes of the Presbytery (published in a limited edition of six) reveals the matrix of marriages and divorces among the Kirks of Glasgow. One of the copies can be consulted in the Presbytery offices built into a city-centre church which is itself a symbol of the fission and fusion process – Renfield St Stephen's in Bath Street. Its constituents number thirteen (Blythswood, Buccleuch, Cowcaddens, Grant Street, Lyon Street, Milton, Port Dundas, Renfield Street, St George's Road, St Matthew's, St Stephen's, St Stephen's West, Shamrock Street).

Away from the centre, the picture is the same. Pollokshields Free Church for instance is now part of one Pollokshields parish which consists of the former East, Glencairn, Kenmure, St Kentigern's, Titwood and West churches. Six in all – a double holy trinity in the fertile crescents of Pollokshields where Islam now is the majority faith and but a muezzin's shout from the new mosque on the banks of the Clyde which caters for the large Asian population which has settled in Glasgow. Scotland has 10,000 Sikhs and 10,000 Hindus, most of whom live in Glasgow, but the Muslim community is the largest – 27,000, of whom the bulk live in Woodlands (where there is an Islamic centre) and Pollokshields. The Jewish community is much older but under 4,000 in number and concentrated on the South side of the city in the Whitecraigs/Giffnock/Newton Mearns area. Surgeon Henry Tankel is its most prominent voice and, the cantor at Newton Mearns, its most tuneful one. But the incomers who created most stir in Glasgow's history were the Irish Catholics.

Following the Irish famines of 1845–50, immigration pushed the Catholic population of Glasgow up to 140,000 by 1878, the year when a Catholic hierarchy was restored to Scotland. Two-thirds of Glasgow lived in overcrowded conditions and there were severe social problems mostly associated with alcohol abuse. The Catholic 'ghetto' was as much a product of Protestant hostility and indifference as Catholic separatism. But not all the aggro came from the Prots. Resentment against the native Scots priests by the immigrants led the pro-Irish newspaper *The Free Press* in 1864 to demand the restoration of a hierarchy of bishops and 'as the people are all Irish, they consider that Irish bishops should be appointed'. Understandably, at the time of the Great War there were fears that the Easter Rising and Republicanism would make itself felt in Glasgow but the Catholic community gave no trouble and the 1918 Education Act setting up a system of state-funded Catholic schools was seen by many as a reward for loyalty to the British state.

The Catholic and Protestant communities live now in much greater harmony in the 'dear green place' but the schools system is a nettle in that ecumenical garden. No political party sees votes in grasping it by abolishing 'sectarian schools' and the very mention of abolition to the Archbishop of Glasgow, the Most Rev Thomas Winning, is like touching his cheek with a nettle. This earthy son of Motherwell will probably soon have a red hat to hide the flush if his dominant leadership of Scotland's Catholics is underlined by making him a cardinal, as many expect. In 1971 as many as

Archbishop Thomas Winning, 1987.

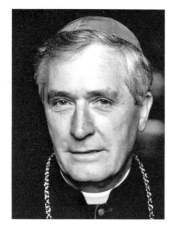

*Son et Lumiere at
Glasgow
Cathedral, 1988.*

*Glasgow's
mosque at
midnight proving
that all that
glitters is not gold
but translucent
plastic, 1984.*

Billy Graham crusade at the Kelvin Hall, 1954.

The Festival of Saint John, 1958.

forty per cent of all pupils in Glasgow's schools were Catholics but falling rolls, closures and defections to the non-denominational system have made this a sensitive issue. Growing evidence that parents are less enthusiastic than their bishops about Catholic schools make the latter nervous that their source of communicants might be dammed. Another sensitive area is inter-church marriages or 'mixed' marriages to use the less polite term. In 1966 twenty-eight per cent of Catholic marriages in Glasgow were in this category. By 1977 it had risen to forty-four per cent and Catholic marriages were a quarter of all marriages in the population. This may help to explain why, despite the substantial numbers who belong to sectarian organisations like the Orange Order, the potential for sectarian conflict has been progressively defused in the city. There are numerous ecumenical projects at local level, but it would be wrong to pretend that relations at a formal level are close. In 1989 a British Council of Churches report noted that 'there is no Glasgow city-wide Council of Churches and no forum for mission reflection for the whole city though the potential exists for this, because church leaders meet regularly with representatives of the Strathclyde Regional Council (at the Council's request) and beforehand they gather to prepare for the meeting.'

Until recently Scottish and Glaswegian Catholicism was among the more conservative brands in Europe (which is not surprising considering its Irish origins) but there were few takers for the Tridentine Mass movement when it began. A posse of Lefèbvre devotees took over a former Free Presbyterian church in Renfrew Street in 1985 but got off to a sticky start when it was discovered that their 'priest' was not validly ordained.

Extremists at the other end of the religious spectrum can find their needs catered for by Pastor Jack Glass in the Zion Sovereign Grace Baptist church in Polmadie where they can hear blood curdling doctrines of predestination roared at full tilt. The Pastor's profile is out of proportion to the number in his flock, of a hundred or so, but he is scathing about proselytising crusades offered by well known 'liberals' like Rev Ian Paisley (who is often a guest in Glasgow of the Jock Troup Memorial church) because they permit their converts to make a decision to be saved (the elect are selected, not self-elected, says the Pastor). Another version of this is preached by the Rev Donald MacLean, Grand Inquisitor of the Free Presbyterian church in Woodlands Road and scourge of Lord Chancellors.

The 'Good Church Guide' to Roman Catholic churches in Glasgow might list the following: St Aloysius in Garnethill – Jesuits, robed choir and upmarket liturgy plus the chance on the Feast of St Blaise (3 February) to get your throat blessed between two candles. Less dangerous is the summer festival of blessing the lilies which occurs across the river in the Franciscan 'cathedral' of St Francis in the Gorbals attended by thousands. The real Cathedral in Clyde Street (St Andrew's), of which we have already heard, caters for early morning confessions from seven forty-five on and a 'One O'Clock Gang' for lunchtime mass, and is reflected in the glassy splendour of the new Archdiocesan offices (teasingly christened Marcinkus Mansions because they contain the archdiocese administration in a more economic form but cost almost as much as the £4 million deficit which it is carrying). Another popular venue for the faithful is the Passionist Order's church of St Mungo's at Townhead just off the motorway. For sheer speed, however, St Alphonsus in London Road caters for the convenience of visitors to the Barras. The title of 'fastest mass in the west', though, probably belongs to Father Tierney, of St Simon's in Partick, whose machine-gun delivery attracts attendances several times the size of his parish roll. St Peter's, Hyndland

Street, probably wins the prize for the prettiest Catholic church.

In Protestant Kirks, aesthetics are less in evidence, but the splendour of the aforementioned church in Pollokshields is undoubted. Govan still captures a little of the 'Glory of God in the High St'. It was built just over a century ago in the time of Dr John MacLeod who was followed by his nephew George in a Kirk dynasty which is as impressive as the liners built in the sight of its spire. The Grecian nobility of Wellington on Gilmorehill opposite the University stands as a gravestone to the great temples of star preachers but with a rumoured half a million pounds needing to be spent on it, may be more of a millstone. Fundamentalist evangelical preaching centres on St George's Tron and Sandyford Henderson whose pulpits still echo to the sound of certainties but even in the well-attended suburbs of Newlands South or Netherlee the erosion in church attendance is biting. The Cathedral, where it all began, is certainly not immune from that process, but the three-million-pound Cathedral Square project which will include a restaurant and mini-theatre is making sure that the Cathedral building, which is owned and maintained by the Crown, remains the jewel among Scotland's churches.

IAN PAUL

Sport in Glasgow

THE VOLATILITY OF THE PLACE AND THE STUBBORN HONESTY OF ITS citizenry have ensured that sport in Glasgow has enjoyed and endured a parallel image to that of the city itself. As with the other faces that Glasgow shows the world, sport has been unable to hide, or even disguise, the warts, but it would be fair to say that, in a city dominated by football giants Celtic and Rangers, papering the cracks might have daunted Michelangelo.

Yet it would be wrong to assume that the unhealthy, repugnant bigotry which masquerades under religious banners when these two teams, known as the Old Firm, get together, is a true reflection of the city's attachment to sport. Much more accurate would be the picture of the raggedy urchins kicking a piece of cloth around gas-lit streets. As with the image of the Brazilian waif dazzling on the beaches of Rio, there is – or at least was – much truth in the vision of Glasgow's young men being totally obsessed by the sport which, within its borders, was undoubtedly the people's game. Even if the advent of rival attractions has reduced the number of street stars, there is still no subject, even the weather, which is discussed with such commitment . . . *ad infinitum*. In days of not so long ago the shipyards, the factories would resound with argument, and if there are more chartered accountants than plumbers involved today, the debate is no less heated.

It is that inexplicable fascination with football which might be a better representation of the city's predominant sporting bent, a devotion which is mirrored in the very presence of its oldest club, Queen's Park, which began as a club for amateurs in the nineteenth century and remains amateur today, a glorious anachronism in a sport that has become the epitome of professionalism. The fact that the Spiders, for that is their nickname, are alive and kicking reasonably well even yet says much for their own traditional application but much, too, for the city's appreciation of values long since erased. It was far different in Queen's early days when, as one of the first clubs founded in Britain – established in 1867 – it very nearly won the FA Cup and did win the Scottish Cup ten times between 1874 and 1893. It was due to Queen's influence that Scotland became the fanatical football nation of the last hundred years, for which some of its less committed citizens might not be eager to offer thanks. At one stage after Queen's example had been set, Glasgow boasted thirty-five teams and even after senior levels were properly established and the game grew up, Glasgow supported six senior sides for most of this century.

Besides the Old Firm and Queen's, Clyde and Partick Thistle have soldiered on with their minor, but welcome, contributions to the great football adventure. The one name missing from relatively recent club lists is that of Third Lanark, founded as the Third Lanark Rifle Volunteers in 1872, which was mismanaged and manhandled into liquidation in 1967. Its demise was a great disappointment to southsiders who saw the Thirds as the bastion of neutrality between the Greens and the Blues. It is a role that Thistle, too, has tried to fulfil. The Jags, one of the easier football nicknames to understand, have excited a great deal of sympathy, even emotion, in their

Rangers versus Celtic at Hampden, 1965. Ritchie punches clear with McKinnon and Lennox jumping.

long history (Partick Thistle was launched in 1876) but much of that might have to be called cupboard love. It is only when the team from Maryhill – which moved there from nearby Partick in 1933 – becomes involved in a game of some importance that the closet Thistle supporters emerge on to the Firhill terracings.

Clyde, too, has been much loved by a loyal, if small, band of followers, even if their devotion was severely tested a few years ago by the loss of its home ground, Shawfield. However, in Glasgow's football story, these clubs, worthy though they are, can only be bit players. It is the fanaticism that surrounds the other two which has made the real impact, not all of it bad. If the infamy that the tribal behaviour has earned the city could have been done without, the corollary has sometimes been worthwhile in football terms at least. The standards set by the clubs from the south and east of the city have led the way in Scotland, and not infrequently Britain. If Rangers has always been the bigger club, in resources and support, with devotees around the globe, Celtic brought the city into genuine world-wide spotlight when it won the European Cup in 1967, the first British club to do so.

The closeness of their rivalry has been remarkably enduring. At the time of writing, Rangers had won 39 League titles, Celtic 35, but in the Scottish Cup Celtic had been successful 28 times against 24 by the team from Ibrox. They first came together on 29 May 1888, when the newly formed Celtic played its first official match against Rangers which had been well established, having been around for fifteen years. Celtic won that 'friendly' and the teams spent much time in the early days playing each other on that basis. Whatever else their confrontations in modern times can be called, the first word to come to mind is not 'friendly'. Yet it is this intense rivalry, seen by many of the fanatics as the manifestation of the Protestant-Catholic differences recalled and recorded by generations since the Reformation, which contributes to what is sometimes called 'the greatest club game in the world.'

The changing attitudes in Glasgow, the gradual retreat from the old entrenched hatreds and the strictly professional, businesslike approach of the clubs – vis-à-vis Rangers' highly publicised signing of a Catholic – may all help, in due course, to bring about the erosion of the bigotries. The fact is, nevertheless, that the great majority of Glasgow people have refused to have anything to do with the nonsense that has prevailed on some of these occasions. It might have been inevitable that, in a city with such a passion for the game, there would be the occasional explosion of violence, especially when the Celtic genes are inclined to spawn tempers as short as the men themselves. Glaswegians have never been renowned for reticence when the duelling glove lands at their feet and such willingness to stand up and be counted – counted out, often enough – is perhaps the reason that in the rough old world of fisticuffs, the wee men from the city have done rather well.

Names like Elky Clark, one-time British and European fly-weight champion, Peter Keenan, bantam-weight champion of Britain and Europe, and Jim Watt, world lightweight champion, have become familiar around the world's boxing rings. If Watt, the articulate, bright young man whose exploits packed the Kelvin Hall and Ibrox stadium in the seventies and eighties, represented the post-war Glasgow generation, better educated and better fed, the most legendary boxing son of the city, Benny Lynch, epitomised the flawed brilliance of the Glaswegian of the pre-war era. Gifted, self-destructive, outrageously generous and incorrigible, Lynch, who became champion of the world at flyweight, fulfilled all the requirements

McInnes (Third Lanark) about to pass before being intercepted by Kilmarnock right-back, Richmond, 1961.

of the archetypal Glasgow hero. Perhaps some of those endearing qualities would be recognisable in the only bigger man Glasgow has produced to make a real name in the fighting business. John 'Cowboy' McCormack was a middle-weight of immense talent who, perhaps with greater application, would have improved even upon the British and European titles he won.

The obsession with football and the attraction of boxing, from whose booths so many Glasgow working (and non-working) men emerged with a few bob earned for what they might do for fun of a Friday night, were easy to understand in a city that has long been recognised as a bastion of what they themselves would call the working class. Yet while those sports undoubtedly captured the interest of the great majority there was still a sizeable community who were having their fun at sports which many of their peers would have disregarded as pastimes for the rich. Rugby has survived and thrived in the city for as long as its professional cousin, football; and cricket, that English game, has been in town just as long, probably longer. The proponents of these games – many hundreds of them every week participate in and around the city – would not suggest that there is any comparison between their favourites and the association game in its magnetic appeal for Glaswegians but they have every right to point to their sports' longevity as evidence of a far greater attraction than many citizens would wish to concede.

If rugby's initial appeal was to schoolboys of similar ambitions as William Webb Ellis, the Rugby School chap who picked up the football and ran, thus initiating what was to become the oval ball game, its endurance has to be due to much broader acceptance. There is no record of a Scottish Ellis doing a runner but rugby as he devised it was spotted in Scotland in the mid-nineteenth century, and it is certain that, with Edinburgh schools' example, some Glasgow education establishments followed suit. The first senior clubs were comprised of players from former pupils sides and universities. When the West of Scotland club, whose ground, Hamilton Crescent, has played a particularly influential role in sport in the city, was founded in 1865, emerging as an off-shoot of the cricket club of the same name, there were plenty of former pupils of various schools looking for the opportunity to continue playing the game they had enjoyed on their playing fields. A number of former Glasgow High School pupils joined West, for instance, before the High formed its own club in 1884. Even more went to West when the High School disbanded two years later but happily revived in 1889 and is with us still, having amalgamated with Kelvinside Academical in 1982, a club which has also been around for more than a century. The amalgamation was considered judicious because of the preponderance of clubs – five – around the West End of the city, itself an indication of the game's popularity with a sizeable number of young men. Today there are twenty-eight senior clubs in the city, many more youngsters from outwith the public school system taking part than before, and as keen a rivalry as ever existed in the association game. That rivalry, in the best traditions of amateur sport, is just as keen on the cricket field where a whole collection of Glaswegians pass their weekends.

One man generally given credit for helping to popularise the game of cricket in and around the city was a Glasgow businessman, Colonel David Buchanan, who was the first West of Scotland club president and who is believed to have helped most clubs in the area financially in those pioneer days. Among them was the Clydesdale club which had been in existence since 1848. Today there are about twenty-four clubs enjoying the sound of leather on willow . . . and some of their members openly admit it.

Celtic fans celebrate a 3-0 victory over Dundee, 1988.

In a city where the ability to run fast was in-bred as a necessity for some to escape the Polis, it should be no surprise that athletes and athletics have been an integral part of the leisure life. The great regret for many of us is the passing of the marvellous Ibrox Sports and other superb athletic events which took place at the major football grounds. Their going has not coincided with a lessening of enthusiasm for the running, jumping and throwing business. On the contrary their increasing attraction has been emphasised by recent events, such as the custom-built indoor arena at Kelvin Hall, the first such facility in Britain. It was there that the first triangular match between Britain, Russia and the USA was staged in 1989 – Britain won – and it is there that the European Championships will be held in March 1990. With more than twenty athletic clubs in the area, it is hardly surprising that the Glasgow marathon proved popular but its appeal for the masses initially was staggering, and not just literally. The People's Marathon, as it became known, established itself in the eighties as the third largest in the world, behind London and New York. City clubs have spawned some fine athletes, among them Frank Clement, the superb 1500-metre runner, and high jumpers Alan Paterson and Crawford Fairbrother. The great Moroccan, Said Aouita, even made his first international appearance in the cross country World Championships in the city in 1978 when he finished thirty-seventh, the Scottish mud proving too much for the man who was to become arguably the finest all-round runner in history.

Golf fanatics abound in a town where municipal and private clubs provide opportunity to tackle that most infuriating and satisfying of games. From Haggs Castle in the south, where the first Glasgow Open was staged, to Cawder in the north, venue for the Scottish Women's Open, there are hackers and hotshots galore. Some sports die and are reborn, like speedway, others soldier away as enthusiastically as ever until they are 'discovered', like basketball, and yet others are newly born, like American football. If speedway's halcyon days were in the immediate post-war era the bikers have shown a remarkable durability. Glasgow Tigers have moved around the central belt with amazing adaptability, from the original White City, in town, to places like Ashfield, Coatbridge, Blantyre, and at one point Hampden Park. At the last count, they were based in the city again, at Shawfield, aiming to thrill another cinders generation.

They do their dusty business in the same stadium that has housed the great army of greyhound racing fans who for generations have eyed those bookmakers' boards with misplaced optimism. At one time the city boasted six booming tracks but apart from Ashfield, the most durable of the flapping tracks, Shawfield now hosts the only National Greyhound Racing Council action in town but even that is only thanks to a rescue act after the stadium was closed in October 1986. For seven months the hare stayed switched off but a consortium eventually managed to rewire the plug and they were off and running, to big crowds, once again.

They will no doubt carry on racing and biking at Shawfield until the next century, an era which sport in Glasgow approaches with justified optimism. There may be exciting days ahead for the new arrivals. How much ground, for example, will the Yankee grid iron game gain as television, perhaps sport's finest and most terrifying publicist, continues to make even its esoteric complexities almost comprehensible? What is for sure is that the rugby players, who will remain amateur at club level, whatever happens to the internationalists, the cricketers and the myriad other fanatical participants will go on doing their own thing to their delight and the great

Dave McParland and his Partick Thistle players celebrate their Second Division championship, 1971.

*Ibrox Park, home
of Rangers
Football Club,
1989*

Glasgow Rangers' Terry Manghum tries a shot at the basket.

Clydesdale's batsman Sandy Strang expresses his disbelief, 1986.

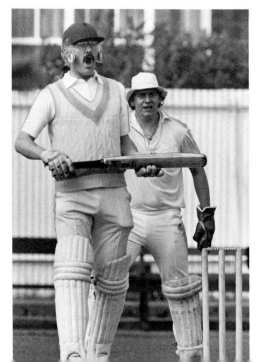

Iain Nelson of Glasgow Diamonds is brought down, 1988.

Matt Duncan of West of Scotland shows anguish as his pass is intercepted, 1988.

*Glasgow
speedway, 1988.*

*Greyhoud racing,
Shawfield, 1984.*

Benny Lynch
being filmed at
Shawfield Park,
1935.

Jim Watt has just
retained his
world
light-weight
crown at Ibrox
Park against
Howard Davis,
1980.

pleasure of those who follow, follow. Which brings us back to where we started, among those warts.

If there is to be a modern football home for the Scottish International team, I would prefer to see it at a revamped Hampden, in Glasgow where the true heart of the game lies. Its steep slopes are king-sized memory banks for the majority of the male population within the city borders, and beyond, and the continuity of that tradition would be welcomed by the sentimentalists among us.

Great things are about to happen in the People's Game and it would be unthinkable if Glasgow were not to be part of the European super plan which seems likely to be fathered in the near future. The twin giants at Ibrox and Parkhead, with all their flaws, will want to be part of that strategy. In that prospect, perhaps, lies the most exciting hope for the citizens who have endured the embarrassment occasioned by the insular rivalry. On the broad continental stage, where the Juventuses, Bayern Munichs, Barcelonas and Real Madrids seek the spotlight, there is not a lot of time wasted on determining whether you are a Billy (Protestant) or a Tim (Catholic).

Jack Milroy and
Rikki Fulton as
Francie and Josie.

Tommy Lorne,
1933.

ANDREW YOUNG

Entertainment/Showbiz
in Glasgow

WHAT'S ENTERTAINMENT? ACCORDING TO THE WORDS BY HOWARD DIETZ, put to the music of Arthur Schwartz, for the MGM musical *The Band Wagon*:

> Ev'rything that happens in life can happen in a show
> You can make them laugh,
> You can make them cry;
> Anything, anything can go.

Entertainment can mean so many things to so many people. You know when you meet it because you are enriched by the experience, although you may not be able to say exactly why. One thing is for sure: entertainment is international and in the year 1990 people from abroad will be enriched by what Glasgow has to offer across the whole spectrum, of drama, music, comedy, opera, ballet, street scenes and even, perhaps, football.

It is only when you start to think about it that you realise in how many forms that which can be classified as entertainment can be found in this city. Equally, the people who live in Glasgow and the whole of Scotland will be entertained by great artists coming in from all over the world. It is a time to forget the stupid rivalry that is stirred up by mischief-makers between Glasgow and that other great culture capital – Edinburgh. We should get on with the show and forget the inter-city niggling. What better year to nurture a spirit of co-operation?

'The clown with his pants falling down, Or the dance that's a dream of romance . . .' The initial reaction to the word entertainment is to think of comedy. In this division Glasgow and the west of Scotland has always had a reputation of, dare I say it, not only smiling better but laughing better, too, because it is an area that has thrown up so many natural entertainers. The mask of comedy is the opposite of the mask of tragedy and, before these more enlightened times there was a much greater need for the antidote of laughter to counteract the industrial squalor in which so many lived.

The list of comedians whose reputations will be forever part of Glasgow's history goes on and on. To my regret I never had the privilege of seeing Tommy Lorne whose theatrical home was the old Princess's Theatre, now the Citizens', nor did I see Frank and Doris Droy at the Queen's, or Will Fyfe. But I will never forget many of the others, like Dave Willis, whom I would regard as the funniest natural comic in the world. Or George West who followed in Lorne's footsteps, Jack Anthony, Alec Finlay, Tommy Morgan, Jack Radcliffe, Lex McLean, Billy Rusk, Johnny Beattie. The late Duncan Macrae and the present Una McLean, both gifted actors, too.

Jimmy Logan, a comic and an actor, emerged from the Logan Family act at the old Metropole, and was to go on and triumph in the role of Archie Rice, created by John Osborne and most successfully portrayed by Laurence Olivier in *The Entertainer*. And, of course, no history of the Glasgow comedy scene would be complete without Rikki Fulton and Jack Milroy who can

Duncan Macrae, 1961.

*Dave Willis
among the girls,
1959.*

work individually or as the double act, Francie and Josie.

In Glasgow there is a special ethnic comedy, some of which would not travel well, does not choose to travel, but which can still be appreciated by visitors from all over the world in much the way they might appreciate a local wine in a French province (only in this case, make that Scotch). In last year's (1989) summer show at the King's, there was a South American speciality act, the members of which did not speak English, but they would stand at the side of the stage every night watching Fulton and Milroy as Francie and Josie and one of them told Fulton (in Spanish): 'We could not understand a word you were saying, but you were very funny.'

Fulton puzzles over the question, what's entertainment? 'It's like trying to define humour. I don't know. It's obviously a form of relief from everyday routines and work and worry, where particular, unusual skills are shown and enjoyed by the people seeking that relief. And when it works, there is no mistaking it. Audience and artists become members of the one family.' Even the Master, Noel Coward, who often stood on that same King's Theatre stage, did not delve into hidden reasons for success, merely acknowledged in the title of his autobiography that he had *A Talent to Amuse*.

I have been speaking about the old troupers and it has been suggested that there is no one waiting in the wings to replace them. Nonsense! The Glasgow comic genius will always find an outlet. Humour is a reflection of the times, and today we have new talent in people like Craig Ferguson, Victor and Barry, Arnold Brown, Gerry Sadowitz, as well as the comedy acting talent equally at home on stage and television. For this Colin Gilbert's comedy unit at BBC Scotland TV should be praised.

Many of Glasgow's most successful entertainers came through the time-honoured natural grading system which decreed: Either give the audience what it wants or get off the stage. Cruel but effective. At the old Panopticon Theatre in the Trongate where Stan Laurel first trod the boards, the orchestra pit was covered with wire mesh so that the musicians would not get hit by rivets intended for the 'artistes'. It was here, too, that Jack Buchanan, one of the most sophisticated entertainers of all time, also survived this form of instant criticism.

It is only in recent years that Glasgow has had a school which can develop the natural talent of would-be entertainers. Referred to grandiloquently as 'Scotland's national conservatoire for the performing arts,' the Royal Scottish Academy of Music and Drama has now been re-established in magnificent new premises in Renfrew Street, just round the corner from the Theatre Royal. Edward Argent, Director of the College's School of Drama, lists a few former students who have gone on to entertain to critical acclaim – classical actors such as Ian Richardson and Iain McDiarmid, stars of stage and screen like Hannah Gordon, Tom Conti, Bill Paterson, John Cairney and Phyllis Logan; Andy Stewart, Una McLean and John Grieve. Another old boy, David Hayman, has moved from acting (*A Sense of Freedom*) to directing Martin Sheen in London's West End, and is now artistic director of 7:84 Scotland. The school's contribution to 1990 events includes hosting an international conference of European drama colleges, the first of its kind; also, a special series of public Masterclasses, a familiar concept in music, but new in theatre. The idea had a brilliant beginning last year when Prunella Scales gave two demonstrations of how to combine erudition and practical teaching skills with the entertainment.

Across the River Clyde, located in a cultural pillbox in the Gorbals, is the hugely successful Citizens' Theatre. It has established an international reputation under its Artistic Director Giles Havergal. It took on a new life nearly twenty years ago with the arrival of Giles. The Citizens' is certainly not in the concept of cosy, traditional theatre, but it obviously passes the entertainment test because it plays regularly to full houses. It has established its own individuality and character, keeping its home in Glasgow, very much in the same way as Alan Ayckbourn has established his roots in Scarborough. Housed in one of the few surviving buildings left in the old notorious Gorbals, it makes the occasional sortie outside of Scotland, but, for the most part, gets on with its mission in Glasgow while the London critics come to it.

'Entertainment is something that I possibly see from a different angle,' says Havergal. 'I remember being asked: Do you think theatre should be there to entertain or to instruct? Is it meant to be just pap to entertain you, or is it meant to be something more? My reply is that, in order to entertain, it has to do both, and I suspect the word entertainment has come to mean being entertained by something mindless. Whereas, to be really entertained, you've got to be pleased, but there's got to be an element of being told something you don't know in order to enhance your experience. I think this even goes for sport – when you're watching an extremely well-played football match, your understanding of human capacity, of human endurance and so on is extended . . . I think it would be absolutely terrible in the theatre if all we did was instruct. Somebody once said that if you just entertained or just instructed it was like playing on either the white notes or the black notes of the piano, but not both. I think to entertain is to do something quite profound to somebody. Because it is through a pleasurable experience that you expand their knowledge.'

Over the years there has been considerable success at the Citizens' with plays by Brecht, plays that could be extraordinarily boring. Havergal thinks this success has been due to the fact that they had seen the kind of entertainment aspect contained in the text and hadn't performed the plays as a kind of dour memorial to Brecht. There was a lot of humour, because Brecht was a very funny man. He thought their productions worked because, in John McGrath's phrase, people knew they would have a good night out – have something to make them laugh, something to make them cry, and something to make them think.

Havergal sees a general revival on the Glasgow theatre scene. While there had been more theatres thirty years ago that had since been pulled down, other smaller theatres had taken their place – the Tramway, the Mitchell, the Tron. 'I know there are nights in Glasgow when every single theatre is full. That's marvellous. That's entertainment.'

Michael Boyd, Artistic Director of the Tron, which is located in an ancient church hall right in the heart of Glasgow, uses different words, but says roughly the same as Havergal. One kind of entertainment, he says, is the transporting delight that takes you outside of yourself, shakes you, tickles you, makes love to you . . . and then dumps you. And there's the other kind, that you bring to yourself, that demands that you make sense of it in terms of yourself. At the Tron they try to marry the two. At the Tron they have done the lot – the Five Past Eight-type variety show, the gang show – shades of the old Panopticon which was in the next block – plus the questioning drama. 'Our very serious concern here is that they shouldn't necessarily be separate issues,' he says.

The late Victorian Theatre Royal, which was miraculously rescued from the devouring jaws of television – STV had converted it as their HQ before getting a custom-built place next door – is the home of Scottish Opera and provides a Glasgow stage for Scottish Ballet, plus many visiting forms

Jimmy Logan, 1988.

Craig Ferguson, 1985.

of entertainment. David Jackson, who for fourteen years was manager there believes the word entertainment would be applied more to musical presentations such as *Kiss Me Kate, Song and Dance* and probably Gilbert and Sullivan. Also to light plays and popular ballets, jazz concerts and middle-of-the-road bands, rather than opera, classical concerts, contemporary dance or Shakespeare. But he says that Shakespeare himself, and, indeed Mozart and Puccini, would agree that they were working in the equivalent in their time of the entertainment business.

Scottish Ballet, which started off as the Western Theatre Ballet in Bristol before being located in Glasgow by its founder Peter Darrell, is by happy coincidence, celebrating its twenty-first birthday in May 1990, an occasion it means to celebrate in a big way. The Ballet's Chief Executive, Peter Kyle, says he feels they are not élitist in any way and have an extraordinary range of works in their repertory, from the white classical ballets, like *Swan Lake*, to the dramatic works created by Darrell. Also the hugely vigorous productions like *Romeo and Juliet* which swing from street circus and carnival at one extreme to the pathos of the tomb scene at the other.

Cameron McNicol, who has come home from managing the Albert Hall in London, to be Director of the new Glasgow International Concert Hall, like Giles Havergal, believes that football is entertainment – 'In my book entertainment would include the widest form of cultural and sporting populism. I think the concert hall is a major statement of Glasgow's cultural renaissance and will be seen and heard in that way for many years.'

DAVID BELCHER

Youth Culture

BEWARE, CHILDREN, OF THOSE WHO WOULD ADOPT THE AUTHENTIC, multi-hued mantle of cred and try to tell you where to go in pursuit of the hippest, hip-hoppiest pleasures after sundown. Shun those who would claim to know what's ah, shakin' out there on the street and on the dancefloor, who would insist that they are in tune with 'The Kids'. Anyone who claims to be able to tell you all about all the clubs has obviously not been enjoying himself in any of them sufficiently enough to know whether or not they are worth attending. Me? I'm just going to give you a few gnomic pointers: like most of the rest of 'The Kids', I spend the bulk of my time re-inventing myself at home in private, not paying £5 admission to try and do it in public, in the dark, over someone else's choice of pounding beat. Bomp-bomp, bompitty-bomp, excuse me, I feel my head spinning . . . spinning . . .

Glasgow's Miles Davis: there isn't one, we'd have told him to learn how to play in tune. Glasgow's Miles Kington: nope, there isn't one of those, either, far too consciously-absurd and clever-clever. Glasgow's Miles Better . . . ah, yes, my head is clearing and I remember that line from somewhere . . . what does it mean again? While the city of Glasgow is in many and varied ways miles better than it was (rather than actually being better than everywhere else), in what might be termed youth culture (whatever that is), Glasgow is simply miles better than most places in the rest of Britain, outside London.

If youth culture is how young people address one another, dress, enjoy themselves, measure one another, chart their aspirations, articulate their desires, and pretend to be more youthful than they are, then Glasgow has got a lot of it. Not the most inventive, innovative, or original brands of youth culture, but lots of it, lots definitely and derivatively if not definitively, most of it music-related. Glasgow presently likes to think of itself, with some justification, as Rock City, UK. To employ rockbiz parlance, Glasgow-based bands such as Wet Wet Wet, the Blue Nile, Deacon Blue, Hue and Cry, the Silencers, the River Detectives, and Texas, have all, along with emigrés like Simple Minds, done mega business in the charts.

Shoals of less-well-known Glaswegian bands, some signed to big labels, some desperately trying to be, wait in the wings. In turn, posses of London A&R men, lured by the city's track record and by its relaxed all-day drinking hours, visit Glasgow with a regularity much envied by groups from other British cities. Within the last ten years a working music business infrastructure of studios, venues, and rehearsal rooms has arisen. Groups need no longer be forced inescapably to re-locate in London to further their careers.

Quite why there are so many bands from Glasgow, more bands than from any other UK city of comparable size, is one question (as is their quality): what is indisputable is that rock music, live or recorded, plays a vital practical role in the city's perception of itself and in its cultural identity. We rock, therefore we do not have to seek unavailable joinery

Queue for Simple Minds tickets at Barrowland, 1982.

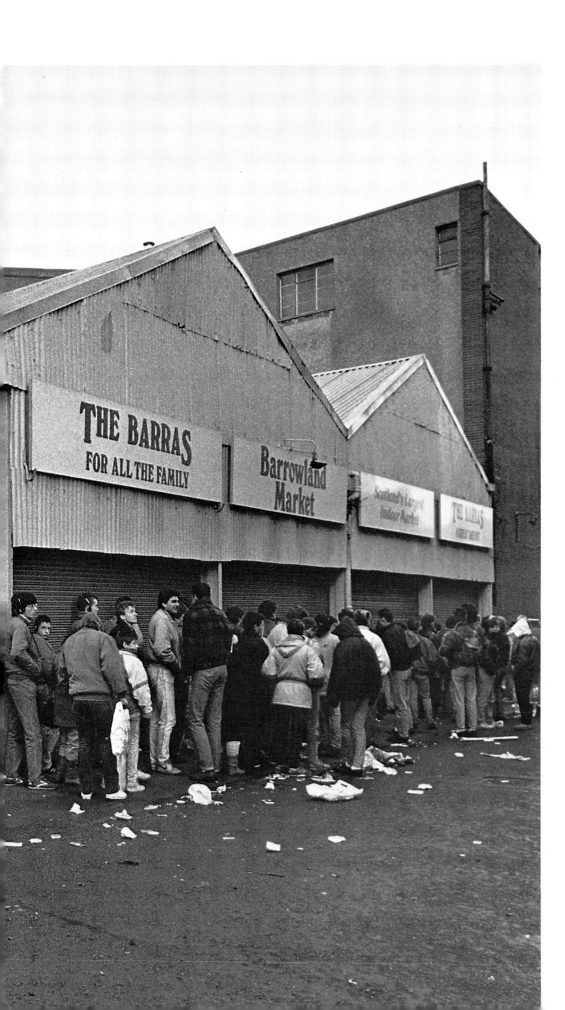

*Jim Kerr of
Simple Minds,
1986.*

Wet Wet Wet,
1989.

apprenticeships which we did not want in any case. We rock because we might as well, because in the post-industrial first city of Europe we stand more chance of getting a number one hit single than we do of securing gainful long-term employment as a warehouseman or invoice clerk.

Likewise, we go to clubs on a semi-professional basis. Because they're there. Because we must. Because we might as well. With twenty-odd late-licensed nightclubs to choose from in city-centre Glasgow (and a lot more new ones arriving in 1990), there is obviously plenty of scope for making a disastrous decision. Thus, if your idea of a fun night out revolves around *not* being surrounded by permed footballers and/or lumpen Sharon and Kevins dancing round Sharon's handbag to the strains of Kylie's latest, you'd be advised to select exclusively from the following list of clubs. Most crucially, consult a local black hack driver and ask him which venue he and his fellows habitually refer to as the Titanic: this place in particular is to be avoided.

In contrast, places surely to be sampled are those which are visited by Bobby Bluebell. Bobby Bluebell: once seen, never forgotten. A Glaswegian version of Joey Ramone and formerly a guiding light in the Bluebells, shock-troops in the first wave of Top-of-the-Popping Glaswegian popsters, Bobby Bluebell gets around, checking out bands, sounding things out, nodding his approval. If you see him going into a club check it out. If you see him coming out of a club, check it out. Bobby clubs and gigs hard and assiduously, working at it like it was a job or something.

Yet above all, remember that nothing is fixed, everything changes and that what was cool on a Wednesday night may have become unspeakably dated by Saturday lunchtime, if not sooner. Movements lose momentum; clubs over-reach themselves and fall by the wayside. Where once there might have been kudos in espousing acid house, now there are more credibility points to be had in rooting for alkaline jazz. In the style wars there are many casualties; there may be some hardline psychedelic casuals, but there are always greater numbers of casual followers who melt away. There will always be a rapid turnover of happening clubs and pubs and what follows is an admittedly partial catalogue of night-time *divertissements*.

Looking ahead, the hottest tip for the future is the Shelter, a subterranean air-raid shelter beneath the Atholl Arms (a pub much favoured by STV mediacrats at the top of Renfield Street) which is currently being refurbished as a bar-cum-live music venue and band rehearsal space and due to open before Christmas. More up-market (not to mention above-ground) will be the as-yet-unnamed club scheduled to open atop swank nosherie John Street Jam (Cochrane Street). Additionally, keep an eye on the Renfrew Ferry, an atmospheric new quayside venue which from time to time stages small musico-theatrical events.

Likewise spreading the range of occasional nightlife venues in a bid to emulate the warehouse parties of London and the Home Counties, both the capacious Tramway Theatre (scene of Peter Brook's *Mahabharata*) and the glass-walled Winter Gardens have recently been pressed into service as impromptu acid house palaces. Keep an eye open for fly-posters alerting the fly. Otherwise, right now these are some of Glasgow's more interesting places to see, and, more crucially, be seen in. If you get to some of them at precisely the right instant, who knows, you may see a club and its devotees metamorphose into, or out of, fashion before your very eyes:

Glasgow disco fever, 1989.

Clubs

Pzazz, 21 Royal Exchange Square, 221 5323.
On Fridays and Saturdays Pzazz mutates into Choice, watering hole for Glasgow's self-appointed inner circle of groovers and shakers, and the home of style apartheid: i.e., if you don't look wealthy and blasé enough, you will be refused admission. OK if you don't take it as seriously as it takes itself (and the music can be very, well . . . choice, I suppose) but primarily a place in which to observe wealthy-looking, blasé people who subscribe to Choice's self-deluding credo: 'for the known and soon to be known.' NB a sunbed tan is your best bet in trying to impress the fashion-*gauleiter* on the door.

Fury Murry's, 96 Maxwell Street, 221 6511.
Despite claims to the opposite effect by the disco *cognoscenti*, still ferociously trendy after all these years (well three years at least, an aeon in nightlife terms, which must prove something about the place's efficacy). Wear your bandana and Kickers with pride (and be prepared to be refused admission if you're wearing them on the wrong night, falling foul of the rules of admission and hence failing the hipness test). Likes to think of itself as the most musically-aware of Glasgow's niteries, but can be very drab, aural-wise. Different nights offer different dancefloor beats: Saturday is Slam, providing a soundtrack for young acid casuals to 'go mental' to in their brand-name uniform; Sunday is Underground, a free-form indie night. Monday night's Freewheelin' is presently the most interesting, blending indie faves like Sonic Youth and Dinosaur Jr with Scott Walker and Abba, T Rex with black dance music. Fury Murry's is also a regular halt on the UK-wide live-gig circuit for 'interesting' up-and-coming bands.

Sub Club, 22 Jamaica Street, 248 4600.
'An underground club gone mainstream' just about sums it up. Where once there was freedom from the tyranny of transient fashion and stylish people wore what suited them best, now there are too many nondescript clubgoers, especially on a Saturday. Where once there was an adventurous, unusual mix of music, now there is generally indifference and anonymity. Nevertheless, satisfaction can be obtained if you choose your night with care. Blackmarket on Thursday features a mix of user-friendly dance music; Joy on Friday is likewise; both nights are run by the same omniscient turntable trio who do Slam on Saturdays at Fury Murry's.

Peggy Sue's, 46 West George Street, 332 3000.
'Let's do the disco right here!' Opportunity for would-be nightlife entrepreneurs to run the club of their dreams for an evening (or for as long as they retain the interest of enough paying customers). Clubs necessarily come and go on a highly sporadic basis, but watch out for Hallucination Generation (usually on a Saturday) which boasts a tasteful and thoughtfully-chosen indie/psychedelic/garage punk soundtrack, and the Love Club (Tuesdays), a metaphorical coupling between Elvis and the Soup Dragons and their ilk.

The Venue, 474 Sauchiehall Street, 332 3874.
Defiantly and comfortably down-at-heel, Radio City, on Friday nights, has an endearing anything-goes attitude. If the DJ feels like playing the entire side of a Jimi Hendrix LP without a break, then he jolly well will, so there. He also tends to play a lot of primal rock'n'roll, Suicide and the Stooges, modern cult classics, plus some Doors, a lot of Rolling Stones from the time before the Stones all either died, or got into cricket and bowling maidens over and suchlike. If you feel inhibited about cutting a rug, this is the place wherein your ass will be painlessly freed, allowing your mind

quite naturally to follow.

Riverside Club, 222 Clyde Street, 248 3144.

A romp'n'stomp ceilidh free-for-all for all ages is generally in progress. Friendly, determinedly un-trendy, great fun. The sole drawback is likely to be your tripping over earnest sociologists writing theses with titles like 'Roots music: its causal link to the emergence of nationalism among young people.'

Rooftop, 92 Sauchiehall Street, 332 5883.

Sticky-floored home to the disaffected hordes who dedicate themselves to the indie muse. Dig out your black hair dye, black lace gloves and purple velvet for Friday night – Goth night. Saturday night features a liberating wodge of the less self-conscious, more trance-dance-oriented indie music (Happy Mondays, Stone Roses). 'Robust' (ahem) security staff. Occasional live gigs, too.

Pubs with live music

Fixx, 86 Miller Street, 248 2859.

Premier pub-rock venue. The place in which to hear (if not always see) live Scottish contenders on stage for free. Perennially packed, perennially sweaty, the bar perennially besieged by those aforementioned London record company A&R men: get in now before said London record companies start charging you money to see your local heroes.

Halt Bar, 160 Woodlands Road, 332 1210.

A real pub for real drinkers rather than a purpose-built live venue, the Halt nevertheless stages real rock'n'roll'n'jazz'n'stuff in the form of highly enjoyable *ad hoc* get-togethers by some of Glasgow's less-well-known musical sons and daughters.

Saints and Sinners, 272 St Vincent Street, 221 1124.

Home to brewery-sponsored demo disco, which works like this: aspiring beat combos submit demo tapes, which are then played to the crowd, who vote upon them, resulting in a chart. Ten minutes and you will be frantically trying to work out the answer to one of Glasgow's burning philosophical questions: are home-made demo tapes killing music or do major labels have cloth ears? As you ponder, try to avoid the seething mob of mendicant aspiring beat combos.

Napoleon's, 128 Merrylee Road, 637 5238.

Nice airy pub, some good bands; shame about the UV light which shows up one's dandruff something cruel.

Videodrome, 33/39 York Street, 221 0441.

Good local bands (sometimes) in a small side room thankfully removed from the thronging mass, all of whom appear to share as an ideal of eco-natural radiance those heavily made-up department-store beauticians (if you know what I mean) . . .

Pubs

Rock Garden, 73 Queen Street.

Passably rocky, but passé rockster-type pub hang-out. Probably the only place in Glasgow where Clare Grogan would still be considered a celebrity.

Variety Bar, 329 Sauchiehall Street.

Currently the hot one: traditional-looking pub with heady mix of art students and thrusting yoof TV media types.

Cul de Sac, 44/46 Ashton Lane.

West End's premier bar, bar none. Shame about some of the clientèle. Always packed to the gunwhales with trendsetters trying to ignore one another as ostentatiously as possible.

Nico's, 379 Sauchiehall Street.

Brasserie-type thingie in the Glasgeau nouveau style, but OK despite that.

Music venues

Barrowland, 244 Gallowgate, 552 4601.

Genuinely funky and atmospheric (i.e., fungal, dirty and smelly). The only place in which to achieve an out-of-body experience with big-name bands in Glasgow. Two cavils: inadequate bars and toilet facilities. However, should you have to venture downstairs for bog or beer during a rowdy performance, you will see one of rock'n'roll's great sights, to wit, the door of the ladies' lav slamming noisily back and forward under the combined power of 4,800 jumping feet above it. Prepare to sweat a lot all ye who enter here.

Pavilion, Renfield Street, 332 1846.

Middling-sized, nicely-frayed theatre which has energetically sought to fill the gap left by the demolition of the vast old Apollo, which once stood across the road.

SECC, Finnieston Street, 248 3000.

Soulless aircraft hangar which has gamely tried, failing miserably, to replace the Apollo. The smaller side halls are tolerable, but instead of going to the main 8,000-seater hall you'd be better off staying at home listening to the records.

Others

The Comic Club, Blackfriars, 36 Bell Street, 552 5924.

Fortnightly comedy of an alternative persuasion from Glasgow collective the Funny Farm.

JOHN FOWLER

The Arts in Glasgow

THE MUSE VISITS GLASGOW MORE THAN SHE USED TO, OR SO IT SEEMS.
Thirty years ago Glasgow was a tough, gritty, grubby working place with
a rough-and-ready popular culture which, we hope, has not been stifled by
sophistication, gentrification and the city's recent elevation as a nominated
European city of all the arts. Once we used to build ships and locomotives
and went to work in trams. Now we put houses on the filled-in dock basins
and the tramway shed has become a theatre. But what a theatre! It was
Peter Brook, magus of the contemporary stage, whose genius transformed
a dilapidated building then under the threat of the demolisher's hammer,
into one of the most adaptable and atmospheric theatre spaces in Britain.
Thanks to Brook, the future of the Tramway as a theatre now seems secure.
But there can't always be Peter Brook and his epic *Mahabharata* or his taut
Tragedy of Carmen, and the real test is to come. The Tramway (both as
a theatre and as a symbol of Glasgow's new status in the cultured world)
will survive only if the excitement of the building can be matched by what
is staged there and if audiences take it to their hearts.

Still to come, as I write, is the concert hall under construction at the
tatty end of Buchanan Street as a belated replacement for the glorious St
Andrews Hall which went up in smoke nearly thirty years ago, torched,
we believe, by a careless member of the audience at a boxing match which
someone had the temerity to promote in these incongruous surroundings.
Like its predecessor, the new hall will be home for the Scottish National
Orchestra, a centenarian orchestra now at a peak of performance, due
in part to a dynamic few years with its recent conductor Neeme Jarvi.
Another conductor from abroad, the energetic Pole Jerzy Maksymiuk, has
masterminded an equally remarkable resurgence by the second symphony
orchestra based in Glasgow, the BBC Scottish Symphony Orchestra. Though
originally conceived as a purely radio band, the BBC SSO has in the last few
years increased the number of its public performances and has widened its
repertory considerably.

Also based in Glasgow is Scottish Ballet, the company founded and
inspired by Peter Darrell and dedicated to the presentation of classical ballet
throughout Scotland in spite of being hamstrung by lack of funds; and Scottish Opera, enjoying a period of rich creativity after some creaky years. Both
have shown welcome interest in innovation: the ballet company's staging of
Stravinsky's *Petrushka*, under the guest directorship of Oleg Vinogradov
of Leningrad's Kirov Ballet, is a fascinatingly radical re-interpretation, and
Scottish Opera's revival of Kurt Weill's rarely performed American music
drama *Street Scene*, was a sensational triumph. The question that hangs
over Scottish Opera is common to all of its kind; how can opera, which
by its nature requires large public funding and is expensive, be made
accessible to a wider audience? Constant *Bohèmes* and *Butterflys* are no
answer; what might be more positive would be the development of Scottish
Opera's shoestring travelling offshoot, Opera Go Round. It would be good,
too, if a means could be found of staging contemporary music drama in a

*Interior of
Citizens' Theatre,
1989.*

*Alasdair Gray,
writer and artist.*

Gododdin:
*frenzied action in
a post-
apocalyptic
theme park,
Tramway
Theatre, 1989.*

way that would attract a wider public; and not necessarily on the grand scale that we are accustomed to in the opera house. A sign of the times is the fact that the enterprising Scottish Chamber Orchestra, resident in Edinburgh, has opened a satellite office in Glasgow.

And new music? The doyen of Glasgow composers is Tom Wilson, whose multifarious works include three symphonies, two concertos, many chamber and choral pieces and incidental music for TV. A younger generation is represented by Edwin McGuire, a composer with an individual voice who has successfully synthesised Scottish folksong idioms with a tougher strand of contemporary music. One of his major recent works was the music for Scottish Ballet's full-length dance version of Peter Pan. The most exciting emergent talent is that of James MacMillan, Ayrshire born and Glasgow based, who has received recent commissions in many fields from a variety of Scottish organisations, including works for performance at the London Proms and a piano concerto for the 1990 Musica Nova series; there is also the prospect of an opera in the future.

Scottish theatre has been a sickly growth in the past. In the first half of the twentieth century, Barrie and Bridie (neither of them from Glasgow), looked to London's West End rather than the Scottish stage. Glasgow's theatrical history has been chequered, with its strongest manifestation on the variety stage, a subject dealt with elsewhere in this book. For a few years before the First World War a Glasgow Repertory Company, founded by the Englishman Alfred Wareing, led a fitful and uneasy existence in imitation of Dublin's famous Abbey Theatre, with the aim – as recorded in the *Glasgow Herald* – of encouraging the 'development of a purely Scottish drama by providing a stage and acting company which will be peculiarly adapted for the production of plays national in character, written by Scottish men and women of letters.' From time to time since then that objective, with variations, has been pursued. It is ironical that in the case of the most successful attempt to establish a true Scottish theatre company in Glasgow, with the foundation of the Glasgow Citizens' Theatre in the last years of the war by James Bridie, fame has latterly been achieved far beyond the city by an innovative staging of the classics (albeit often very minor classics – what else to call *No Orchids for Miss Blandish*?) to the exclusion of any Scottish writing apart from the plays of one of its resident directorate, Robert David MacDonald. There is a nucleus of playwrights working in or near Glasgow (unlikely to seek the designation 'men and women of letters') who have achieved some success on the Scottish stage – the poet Liz Lochhead among them – but not at the Citizens'. It is some twenty years since the Citizens', a charming little theatre in the Gorbals which has been lovingly maintained within and is now dignified, after years as a lone outpost standing guard in a desolation of slum clearance, as the focal point in a post-modernist building development, suddenly emerged as one of Britain's foremost exponents of conceptual theatre under its new director Giles Havergal. Civic prudes were shocked in the early years by what they saw (or, more often, by what they heard of indirectly) on stage, but tastes have changed, Glasgow has become more sophisticated, and the Citizens' has become respectable even in the eyes of those who never go near it. Judging from recent productions, the standards have never been higher.

But Scottish writers, Glasgow writers among them, have to look elsewhere to have their work staged. It can be seen at Mayfest, Glasgow's three-week festival of much theatre and a little music, which is a lusty child of the eighties. It finds a stage, too, at the Tron Theatre, a small auditorium

Liz Lochhead, writer.

George Wyllie, creator of the straw locomotive and the paper boat, 1987.

Artist Steve Campbell.

*Artist Stephen
Conroy, 1988.*

*Glasgow School
of Art, 1981.*

created from an early nineteenth-century church by a group of enthusiasts – now a public theatre open to all, with its own occasional company which was invited to premiere a production at the 1989 Edinburgh Festival. The chosen play was a black comedy of greed and exploitation with a contemporary and distinctly local reference by Ian Heggie, who is – along with the multi-talented John Byrne – the most successful of the playwrights with Glasgow connections.

It's tempting to see Glasgow writers – poets and novelists as well as playwrights – as commentators on, and interpreters of, the working-class scene for the benefit of a middle-class readership, but the most significant prose writer, the novelist Alasdair Gray, by no means fits that category, and the most eminent poet, Edwin Morgan, ranges far beyond any narrow geographical or imaginative boundaries. Gray's epic book *Lanark* is a work of strange and idiosyncratic genius (the eccentricity of which is mirrored in its construction; the middle section of the novel came first) and his talent is unique. There is no school of Gray.

But there is James Kelman, an equally distinctive voice who became one of the Booker finalists in 1989 with his novel *A Dissatisfaction* which John Linklater, Literary Editor of the Glasgow Herald, has described as 'a brilliant piece of sustained writing.' Kelman is Glasgow born and bred; William McIlvanney, whose first, highly regarded novel *Docherty* chronicles a narrow world of urban Scotland, hails from Kilmarnock which is just a short drive away from the city.

Pictorially, Glasgow's image in the immediate past has been fixed in black and white by the photographer Oscar Marzarolli and in oils by the painter Joan Eardley, whose waiflike youngsters gaze coolly from the canvas in baggy pants and wrinkled socks. As yet there is no equally telling contemporary view of Glasgow life; the film maker Bill Forsyth has sought locations further afield for his later movies after an auspicious debut with the whimsical That Sinking Feeling.

But Glasgow has found a new eloquence in the world of art, where the phrase Glasgow Boys, once a convenient label for landscapists of a hundred years ago who were influenced by their French Impressionist contemporaries, has been appropriated by a bright new generation of figurative painters, most of whom are graduates of the School of Art.

If not a school, there is a group of young painters who are readily identified with Glasgow. The phrase 'Glasgow Boys' is a convenient label frequently attached to painters of some 100 years ago, most of whom were landscapists influenced by their French contemporaries. Recently the label has been borrowed to categorise a new generation, mostly graduates of Glasgow School of Art, whose work has gained international recognition mainly for the vigour of its figurative painting. This has been a breath of fresh air in a closed world wearying of the astringencies of abstraction and minimalism. The acclaim has been profitable; the musty smell of the garret does not cling to the new Glasgow Boys, some of whose work has fetched staggeringly high prices. Pictures by Steven Campbell, the most prominent among them, hang in prestigious galleries in Britain and America and others, such as the lyrical Adrian Wiszniewski, Ken Currie, painter of Clydeside narrative, and Peter Howson, exponent on canvas of working-class *machismo*, are names to conjure with in the market place, as is the younger Stephen Conroy. Whether this explosion of talent, nurtured by a group of talented teachers and encouraged by an eager market, will continue to reverberate remains to be seen; but the city is a hive of artistic activity and new talent is constantly being discovered and exposed.

Cleaning supervisor, Betty Rowan, gives the Warwick Vase a dusting at the Burrell Collection, 1983.

The 'Last Night of the Proms' for Glasgow's Kelvin Hall, 1985.

How do you measure a city's standing in the world of art? In terms of present-day activity, which is what really matters, Glasgow is second to none, and likes to think of itself, occasionally and perhaps with reason, as Britain's most successful forcing ground of artistic talent. As a storehouse of treasures of the past it is less pre-eminent, but not inconsiderable. The civic collection of old (and not so old) masters at Kelvingrove suffers no neglect: Sunday afternoon at the Art Galleries (always in the plural) is traditionally one of the great social occasions for the people. Kelvingrove has an excellent mixed collection. The building – pink sandstone folly on the outside and ponderous Victorian baroque on the inside – doubles as art gallery and museum, housing exhibits from the natural world (lots of stuffed birds) and ethnology as well as the artwork, a duality which to some extent bears the stigma of the less than metropolitan (though you can by no means say provincial). In the East End of the city, slap in the middle of Glasgow Green (a place that has seen much of Glasgow's history in the making, from riot and execution to James Watt having his brainwave) is the People's Palace, where there is an enlightened policy of collecting or commissioning artwork relevant to Glasgow's working and social life. The Burrell is all-purpose in a different way, being a window display of the eclectic (that is, eccentric) taste of one wealthy collector. Finally, in the year 1990, Glasgow acquires at last a large modern gallery which will be devoted to displaying both changing permanent collections and major visiting international exhibitions, an asset the city has lacked until now, and made possible by the decision to upgrade the burned-out, civic-owned MacLellan Galleries to a much higher standard than before the blaze. It's a lingering cause for regret to Glasgow chauvinists that Scotland's new National Gallery of Modern Art – replacing an inadequate building in Edinburgh – was sited in the capital and not, as seemed possible at the time, in Glasgow. But the Burrell was on everyone's minds and politicians are wary of dispensing too many millions on one place. That's water under the bridge. We can take comfort in the fact that there are numerous places within the city where working artists are creating the art of today; the Print Studio with its handsome new premises, a scattering of workshops – mainly in the East End – and the Scottish Sculpture Studios. The Third Eye Centre is a gallery *cum* arts centre which adopts a progressive and ambitious policy, and where many of the smaller touring exhibitions from Britain and abroad can be seen.

Out of the public gaze stands Glasgow's most distinguished work of architecture, the Cathedral – a modest, soot-stained gothic pile whose glory is its subterranean forest of a crypt (though, too, its plain, high nave has a sombre appealing simplicity). It's a misfortune that the Cathedral was built on a declivity on the banks of the Molendinar (a river now piped underground). Nowadays, though benefitting from a new visitor centre and precinct, it is overshadowed by the massive and obsolescent Royal Infirmary, which dominates the high ground; a rude neighbour, visible proof that insensitive town planning has a history. The modern masterpiece of Glasgow city-centre architecture, Charles Rennie Mackintosh's School of Art, is as likely to be missed by the unobservant eye, though it lies just a few steps uphill from busy Sauchiehall Street. Like the Cathedral, it remains dedicated to the purpose for which it was built, and eager visitors have sometimes been dismayed to find that access is not easy, especially during vacations when the students have departed. In term time the studios, lit by vast north-facing glass eyes, serve as classrooms, heads are bowed over books in the cramped library and the timbered staircase, worn by the tread of several generations, echoes to the feet of hurrying students. Nothing approaching the distinction of Glasgow School of Art was built until the city finally – after decades – got round to finding a suitable home for the collection of miscellaneous artefacts, paintings and sculpture gathered by the shipowner Sir William Burrell and left to his native city with the proviso that it should be displayed only in a fog-free atmosphere. Once Glasgow moved out of the coal fire age and the skies above it cleared, the Burrell Gallery could be built, excitingly and yet harmoniously within city parkland.

It is unfortunate that timorousness or parsimony has afforded Glasgow few modern buildings of merit. Most of the new public or commercial building in the city centre has been dull and meretricious, and the glorious inheritance of the Victorian and Edwardian city has not been matched in the present day, due to a sad lack of courage and imagination. By and large, post-war Glasgow has been content to show its face dull and plain. Ill-conceived housing estates were a short-sighted response to the decaying city's urgent need for renewal, and they have become a breeding ground for social problems. Architecturally (and socially) Glasgow's prime asset was the tenement, a module for living that still has to be bettered. Fortunately the destruction of tenement city has been halted and many of the buildings brought up to modern standards, though not before planners' blitz and planners' blight has laid waste forever to swathes of the old city. The Gorbals has gone, and along with it a vitality which it is proving hard to recreate.

To the Belly Born

WHAT IS A GOURMET? IF THE GUIDE BOOKS ARE TO BE BELIEVED THE perfect gourmet's six most active habits are the pursuit of food and the avoidance of cigarette smokers, dogs, children, muzak and other diners. The only problem with children is that they could be a shrill intrusion on your naughty weekend. As for dogs I had an excellent roast specimen a few years ago in Taiwan. Nothing, however, should be allowed to interrupt the fervent diner. There is even a story of a group at the late lamented Malmaison who asked for the piano to be switched off. Don't shoot the pianist? The perfect gourmet, therefore, is a celibate, cat-loving, tone deaf recluse. Luckily for Scotland's chefs such species are as scarce as oysters in May.

For whatever reason Scotland is a nation of folk who eat out. Since it still tends to be the men who pick up the tab, I may be forgiven for suggesting that the reason is that they know what happens when they eat in. You may well pick up a smart little bottle of château whatever in the sure knowledge that you will be saving on restaurant bills but no amount of mellow fruitfulness will compensate for the overdone steak and armour-plated potatoes or ease the flatulent wound the Scottish housewife can inflict. This is what truly divides us from the European milieu. This is what truly makes us an island nation, unconquered, because our would-be invaders could not stand the thought of Brown Windsor and mutton pies. The fact is, dear friend, our wimmin (sic!) cannae cook. Liberation is little more than a smirk when it comes to the stove they have never been tied to.

When the Trencherman column was born almost a decade ago the Women's Editor of the *Glasgow Herald* (with whom I am still on speaking terms) said that the new Friday Taste Day pages should have more men writing for them. This was because she knew the truth of the old adage that, 'the cook was a good cook; and as cooks go, she went.' We men stay tied to our stoves or our cheque books.

The social morés of dining out have changed over the years but one thing should be made clear from the start – the City of Glasgow has not just arrived at an understanding of fine cooking; we came out of the woad many years ago. In fact what has happened most acutely during the last decade or so is that our interest in fine eating has been revived. Consider this: in the pre-war years Glasgow and the industry-rich bourgeoisie enjoyed a plethora of fine eating houses at the top of the European tree. The number may have been limited, but it was only limited by the fact that an industrial city had a middle-class minority (though even a century ago the working man was eating oysters and steamed mussels along with other molluscs in the East End of the city). The steel barons, the shipbuilders and the ship-owners had invented the coffee-house. Restaurants developed: the One-O-One, the Whitehall and Ferrari. It was not for nothing that British Transport Hotels should choose to establish and maintain their pinnacle of cuisine in the city at the late lamented Malmaison.

Some of these survived the war but patronage was declining for two

*The Ubiquitous
Chip Restaurant,
1982.*

*Jim Wilson at
The Buttery.*

Smiling from the left are Dick Hurran, 'Five-Past Eight' producer, singer Eve Boswell, restaurateur Reo Stakis, Jimmy Logan and Jack Radcliffe, 1959.

Glasgow Herald *celebrated cartoonist Turnbull lends his unique interpretation of Glasgow's culinary tastes.*

reasons; their original patrons were in decline themselves to be replaced by a younger smart-set much influenced by the American way of life. The hamburger had been born, albeit a travesty of the US version. Quick to observe the growing trend Reo Stakis began opening steak houses which brought to the ordinary man in the street the opportunity to dine in 'Sans Souci' style (memories are made of that) at affordable prices. The most popular steakhouse food of the sixties was prawn cocktail followed by steak; to this day these are the two most ordered dishes in British restaurants. By the late seventies a new breed of young creative chefs was appearing, many from what even the French considered the finest training kitchens in Europe, those of BTH, but they had an uphill struggle. They were not fighting against Scottish bad taste but against British and American commercial operations which preached the cause of fast food.

As a quoted critic of the endless array of foodie guide books which appear each year let us say from the start that this is not a guide, though you may choose to use it as such, but rather one man's quest to satisfy the natural need of hunger with something better than the mediocre. It is an essay dedicated to those who live to eat rather than eat to live; it is dedicated to the *bon viveur* – even in these days of yuppie Scotland it is possible for those over the age of twenty-five to enjoy the good life.

If you belong to the particular breed – and there are many north of the Border – who shower disdain on such a quest as in some manner immoral you will probably want to stop reading now but not, I hope, before you've paid to read this far. Why is it that so many are so quick to criticise those seen to be having a good time and sharing the good life? Do they really subscribe to some Calvinistic concept that life should be hard and cruel (and fed by gruel?); that there is virtue in misery or at least in plainness? I must further distress them and declare this essay to be dedicated to the fast, the frivolous, the gadabout, the dandy, the Beau Brummel and the gentleman Jacks – yes, even Jack Mclean, the journalist colleague who gave up teaching because he could never enjoy the slow luxury of the long lunch that cancels the afternoon. We had just such an afternoon together the day he left school, or should I say teaching. He paid. I enjoyed it.

I've lunched like a lord on hot stews in the open air by the side of dust-strewn North African roads. I have dined in the panelled hush of so-called 'Nouvelle Cuisine' establishments and realised that the hush must be because the diners have all been silenced by the apology of a meal being set before them and the lack of apology which ensues when the outrageous bill is preferred with the addition just a mite incorrect. And there is more to food than the cooking of it, and the eating of it. It may well be the most momentary art form of them all, and I incline to the view that food is art and not simply craft when you add in the nuances of the environment in which it is served and the style of its service. That is the theatre of it. Theatre suppers should be banned. The food is the theatre so why not do it the justice it deserves and stay long enough to appreciate and applaud the performance. Have the playwright brought from the kitchen and tell him of your enjoyment or otherwise. Better still, ask to speak to him before you eat. It may upset the head waiter – though it should not – but it is not the head waiter you are going to eat.

Chefs are maestros and primadonnas all; as conceited a bunch of folk it would be hard to find in any other profession bar the bitchiest of them all – no, not the theatre, me dears, but the wine trade. But you can use that conceit to your advantage since the characteristic means that they respond expansively to praise and comment – if they are not maestros and primadonnas they are not chefs and therefore not worthy of a place in this particular theatre-goer's repertoire. And the finest meal? When I find it I shall quest no more and the *Glasgow Herald* can just reprint the same article every week. But I never shall find it since the repertoire knows no end. As in the field of athletics, culinary records are made to be broken. Thank goodness they are, or life would be very boring and I would be out of a job. As they say in journalism, today's newspaper is only tomorrow's fish and chip wrapping – though at Glasgow's finest fat frying emporium, The Philadelphia, which happens to be the one nearest to me in Great Western Road just beside Kelvinbridge, they have achieved the ultimate sophistication of brown paper parcels. In the kitchen they say that a chef is only as great as his last great meal. *Bon appetit.*

And so to dine. But where to begin? Should I attempt 'a best restaurant in Glasgow' only to discover that by the time this book is printed the chef has moved and the place has turned into a national chain burger bar? Instead I shall work at random through the restaurants which Trencherman visits most; not to work but to eat and enjoy.

My most regular shuttle is between five establishments all of which offer vastly different but emphatic ambiences. The Ubiquitous Chip is one of the oldest restaurants under the same ownership in Glasgow. You enter into a cobbled mews, thoughtfully glassed over; this is northern Europe, after all. This was to be the area for the *passeo* until one customer bodily (and boldly) took his table from the restaurant proper which is in the old stable block and placed it in the mews. The table staff are female; worth a second glance. Glance carefully; emancipation arrived a long time ago at The Chip. This is a place of bustle and high spirits; there are often big, jovial party tables. The kitchen still works under the inspiration of Chef/Patron Ronnie Clydesdale but he encourages the brigade to experiment and new dishes regularly appear. Fashion dictates light modern starters like marinated fish. Shellfish for any course is always at a peak of freshness. Ronnie's belief that the old order must not be forgotten means the offal has not gone out of fashion here – a ragout of oxtail for example, though the smashing tripe is becoming more rare, alas. There are real puddings. The wine list is considered one of the finest in Britain with prices from around £6. £40 and up for two. Upstairs the bar and separate dining area serves café food all day – lower prices and you can still drink from that wine list.

Bearsden is a posh commuter ghetto in which sits Restaurant October. One of Glasgow's newest restaurants, it is youthful and fiendishly chic, a *modus operandi* which manager/partner Hugh Macshannon cultivates with humour. Chef/partner Ferrier Richardson is a Frankfurt Culinary Olympics medal winner and the food is serious whilst the clients tend to be frivolous. The decor is smart, French brasserie in style with pale shades and much use of mirrors. A favourite is a teryaki of beef with pungent wasabi served with a rice bowl and chopsticks. A starter might be a steaming bowl of mussels in a light and drinkable liquor. Beware of October's Grand Dessert; a little bit of everything means an awful big plateful but it is a delight to the eye and the tastebuds. Expect to book on Fridays and weekends. Prices for two with two courses, wine and coffee once again around £40 without effort. Choose from the top of the menu and get serious about the wine and prices escalate, but it's worth it.

Slap-bang in the middle of town and the glitzy Merchant City, lying right opposite the City Hall which makes it handy after a concert, is The City Merchant. The Matteo family are a culinary legend in the city and Tony and Linda's latest venture has proved a roaring success. Lunch is the

Café India, 'Uncle' is ready to welcome customers, 1988.

bargain in this quaintly wood-panelled restaurant. Around £4 gets you the set menu. In season this may well include tartan chanterelles picked by the family at their house near Boat of Garten. The serious food appears daily on the blackboard; fish is the name of the game. Loch-fresh scallops, mussels and oysters. All manner of wet fish such as halibut and sea bass. Take it with a saucing but fish such as this deserves to be just lightly pan-fried in black butter. There's the connoisseur's mineral water, Highland Spring, a brief wine list with a few interesting bottles and a *real* expresso machine. They'll serve you morning coffee and afternoon tea. Two people could have lunch with a glass of wine for around £10. A nice touch is that there is no objection to people ordering starter portions of the more exotic shellfish as main courses. Around £35 and upwards for dinner.

Now to a truly womb-like restaurant; a place which can nurse even the most bruised inner man, the coolly elegant Buttery with its coolly elegant manager Jim Wilson. The place and its staff are so damned spruce that I sometimes think the diners should dress up in Victorian dress for the occasion. It is most certainly worth dressing for. A recent change of chef has caused not so much as a flutter in the kitchen. The spinach-wrapped wood pigeon is a signature dish, the soups a light delight and the mussels come with a drinkable liquor. This is the place for the power lunches and smoochy candlelit dinner, though they'll be as happy to serve you a light luncheon at the marble-topped oyster bar. The set lunch is the bargain at around £13. An improving wine list will help you part with in excess of £50 for dinner.

You just want a steak? There is nothing wrong with that and there is nothing 'just' about the variety offered by Mark Lasicha at The Gypsy Baron. Corny name but corn-fed cows. Sod the decor and the location; a 16 oz sirloin costs £5.95. Mark is from Czechoslovakia so the goulash dishes are worth a try. Wine list strong on Eastern European varieties.

SHORT LIST

Style:
The Rusty Pelican provides you with a glamorous room overlooking the river. Seafood is the speciality of Pepe Rodriguez, the Spanish chef. It is arguably the most expensive restaurant in town and it will be very 'in' for the 1990 season. The French restaurant in The Rotunda, once an industrial lift shaft, has had its moments. In its opening months half the population of Glasgow arrived, not to eat, but to tour this two-restaurant and two-bar complex. The Rogano has become an art deco legend. Stick to plain dishes and you should fare reasonably well. Very much a place to see and be seen in. One Devonshire Gardens represents the must luxurious, not to mention decadent, hotel in town. You can watch the tartan yuppies at play in The Penguin Café on the roof of the Princes Square centre and similar antics take place in D'Arcy's in the basement although I think they like it to be referred to as 'the lower ground floor'.

Italian:
There is a plethora of Italian restaurants in Glasgow although sadly the stout peasant cuisine has been mellowed for the local palate. This happened years ago and slowly the message is getting across that we want it da-way-mama-used-da-make-it. Costanzo at Caprese is a *tour de force*; don't go if you don't feel strong. White stucco, aria muzak, mega-bustle and bargain lunches. Good ambience in the evening. The chef has heard

of garlic and olive oil and isn't frightened to use it but if a stranger to the place it is worth telling Signor C that you want it authentic. Mario, in the suburbs of Newton Mearns, can produce the same goods more *pianissimo* at La Vecchia Romagna.

Asian:
Not for nothing could Glasgow be called the curry capital of Europe. For the sheer difference of the places and their cuisine I would nominate Café India and Balbir's India Brasserie. If you told a Glaswegian ten years ago that there was not one but two chic Asian restaurants in town he'd have choked on his lager. Both these places have brought the word 'dining' to eating Asian. You go to them for dinner (or lunch); not for 'a curry'. Bo at Café India is big and beaming; the gentleman in full Kyber Pass regalia on the door is known locally as 'uncle'. If you want something rather special ask for Bo, tell him how much you want to spend, and sit back and marvel at modern Asian cookery. Forget the lager and choose a sharp Alsatian wine, a Retsina or (why not?) a bottle of bubbly. £12 per person would bring you a feast, but you could spend far less. Balbir's graceful room is more discreet and formal. Both he and Bo have their vigorous adherents and it is not for me to pass judgement. I am not going to suggest what you eat since I always spell the names wrong.

Chinese:
In a city awash with Chinese emporiums I can seriously nominate two for authenticity, one of which is rather seriously out of town. First Gerry Wan's Peking Inn in the midst of town. When I recently asked Gerry to provide an authentic Cantonese banquet he went and ordered 'sea slug' from Hong Kong. It doesn't look so bad cooked and on the plate but dear Gerry had to parade one of the beasts in his hand prior to the meal. Some of the guests were less than excited. But, in town, this is the place. Out of town you take yourself to The Royal Garden which sits in a housing estate (albeit yuppie) in deepest Crookfur. This is another place where it is worth deciding how much you wish to spend and then asking Stephen Ho to get on with it. Excellent wine list. Essential to go in a group of at least four so that you can savour the many delicacies.

The Ubiquitous Chip, Ashton Lane (334 5007). *Restaurant October*, 128 Drymen Road, Bearsden (942 7272). *The City Merchant*, Candleriggs (553 1577). *Buttery*, Argyll Street (221 8188). *The Gypsy Baron*, Cheapside Street (221 1727). *The Rusty Pelican*, by SECC (221 5222). *The Rotunda*, by SECC (204 1238). *One Devonshire Gardens*, Great Western Road (339 2001). *The Penguin Café*, Princes Square, Buchanan Street (221 0303). *D'Arcy's*, Princes Square, Buchanan Street (226 4309). *Caprese*, Buchanan Street (332 3070). *La Vecchia Romagna*, 108 Ayr Road, Newton Mearns (639 1162). *Café India*, 171 North Street (248 3818). *Balbir's India Brasserie*, Elderslie Street at Sauchiehall (204 01860). *Peking Inn*, 191 Hope Street (332 7120). *Royal Garden*, Crookfur Shopping Centre, Harvie Avenue, Newton Mearns (639 6261).

JACK McLEAN

The Other Glasgow

ASK ANY GLASWEGIAN OVER THE AGE OF, SAY, THIRTY-FIVE, WHERE HE *comes* from and he will answer you. Partick, he'll say, or Anderston, or Springburn, or Gorbals, he (or perhaps she) will say. Ask the average Glaswegian under that age and he will tell you where he *lives*. There is a difference. The older Glaswegian still thinks of the older Glasgow and where he was brought up: the old slums, the old districts, the old ways even. The younger Glaswegian doesn't even remember the days of the great diaspora of the fifties and sixties. The younger Glaswegian was brought up in the new estates, the new, and now old, housing schemes. The new ways too. Me, I was brought up in Townhead.

Townhead was the oldest part of Glasgow and had damn-near the worst slums. A dark place. Sparse shafts of grimy grass grew in the cracks in the pavements. There was, I remember, a tree outside the Water Department Clerk of Works building. They pulled most of the district down years ago, to nobody's regret, and much of it became motorway. Today Townhead has few inhabitants though the domestic buildings which remain are much refurbished and even desirable. You will hear the word refurbishment often throughout the course of the following and you might even discover 'desirable' from time to time too. Strathclyde University has covered the old Townhead with its campus as well. The district butts on to the edge of the Merchant City.

The Merchant City: this is a new term. It has caught on though, and ordinary Glaswegians now use the title freely and without the self-consciousness which the name but recently possessed. This is where it is fondly imagined that the new better-off professionals live. Where the smart wine bars and restaurants are, with a clientèle in which you find a heady mix of lawyers and advocates in their blacks, journalists, musicians, artists, locals – it seems that the new Merchant City has thrown up what the apologists claim for it. A new and prosperous city, and a new and prosperous set of inhabitants.

A few years back this new prosperity would have sounded not just unlikely: the idea of Glasgow as the European City of Culture would have seemed a heavy satire. Glasgow was the acknowledged slum capital of Europe. It was where the razor gangs came from, and where the football fans hit each other with bottles in dark Gorbals bars. The children went barefoot and danced in puddles of sewage in dank back courts. The above was something of a myth, just as the economic miracle of the last few years is something of a myth.

For not all of Glasgow has been touched by prosperity. Not all of it at all. The dichotomy betwixt the smart wine bars and the splendid shopping malls and the refurbished tenements in which reside the young professionals is more than noted by those who do not enjoy the benefits of a regular wage, or even the benefits of being able to stay in the city centre at all. When the visitors from the South come up to see the city in its Year of Culture they are unlikely to see much of the other Glasgow which rings the city and which smoulders with resentment at the free-spending antics

*Old and new.
Hoganfield
Street, Blackhill,
1986.*

Barlanark.

E/HOUSE-LOYALISTS

*Dunskaith Street,
Easterhouse.*

of the well-heeled of the Merchant City. The visitors from abroad will see nothing of the older, less prominent, districts of a city which once had the right to call itself the Second City of the Empire.

Glasgow was one of the first cities in the world to attempt outer-city municipal housing estates. At first they worked too. Mosspark and Knightswood were models of housing planning in the pre-war years. Suburban and rather garden-city in a muted sort of way, they worked mainly because the tenants lucky enough to obtain a home in these plain but pleasant areas were generally the sort of people who worked hard in the bluff, Calvinistic, Scottish way. The sons and daughters of the original tenants went on to further education more often than not and many of them inherited their parents' council houses for there is none of the snobbery of the South and a 'good' area, council-owned or not, was a desirable one. Mosspark today is quiet and well-run, if a little lacking in vitality and needing, perhaps, a little work done on it. But 'schemes' like these work well. The later schemes did not. The later schemes which came about because of the post-war housing shortages, or because of the lack of foresight of the planners and the paternalistic notions of less-than-informed local councillors. The later schemes which were to provide the same problems of social irresponsibility that the old slum areas had. Glasgow – the other Glasgow – is riddled with the new slums, all of them now in the schemes.

Go on from Mosspark, through the lines of neat privet hedges, and you will come to Pollok. Pollok was once, as all the schemes were, a decent enough place. There was grass and open space and inside toilets. Areas like this were a revelation to the old slum-dwellers, though they missed the old pubs and shops and neighbours and their uncles and cousins in the next street. By the late sixties, though, the vandalism had begun, and the alienation of the young had resulted in the severe gang delinquency which was rife for a period of ten years or more. Pollok was a by-word for what had gone wrong with the housing developments of the post-war years. It was smaller than Castlemilk or Easterhouse, those vast estates the size of whole towns like Perth, where there were no libraries or pubs or even shops and where transport was exiguous or desultory. Pollok was smaller than estates like that where you could understand why things had gone wrong. What became apparent in Pollok was that it didn't matter about the size of the housing development, the size of the problem was always the same.

Taking a look at the older flats in Pollok you can see the root of what went badly wrong. The old flats now lie seedy and depressing, four out of five windows boarded up, filth and litter heaped outside the often smoke-blackened buildings. The very architecture seems impermanent, like temporary housing for wartime refugees, and yet dispiritingly solid and impermeable. As in all these schemes there are the tell-tale signs of dilapidation, not just of building structures, but of society itself. Tattered curtains in the few houses still inhabited, cans and crisp bags in the close mouths where the glue-sniffing parties go on every night. Old women with shabby shopping bags light with the weight of minimal groceries; old men aged beyond their time, their legs shaky with hardened arteries caused by poor diet and excessive smoking and drinking. Hard-faced youngish women clad in expensive off-the-back-of-a-lorry leather jackets, pushing prams with babies with that pinched look which stems from alcohol pregnancy syndrome. Marked across an entire wall is the graffiti with which the young dispossessed mark out their paltry identities.

*David McKenzie,
Possil.*

Glasgow 'gang',
Nightmare Alley,
Calton, 1976.

It is not all like that. Round the corner from this incubus, in the Linthaugh Road, you will find new private housing being built, even new council housing. A large number of the old flats have been refurbished to a level surprising to anybody who ever saw the old Pollok of even five years ago. The authorities have done a great deal to improve all their housing areas and Glasgow is a wonder to the rest of Europe in this respect. Whether this astonishing improvement can make any lasting difference in an area where unemployment can go as high as fifty per cent and more is another matter.

Further up the road is Nitshill. Between both areas is a drab open country interspersed with electricity board outhouses and inconsequential, out-of-place Shell garages. Nitshill looks the same as Pollok only smaller and more East European. In the best-known pub – The Royal Oak – you will find a cheery enough welcome from the staff and customers. One of the customers, James Barratt, was once the manager here. Now retired, he spent twenty-eight years behind the counter in this very pub and his son Tommy has taken over from him. James sees this continuity as right and proper but points out that it goes unrecognised by the district authorities. 'The people here are rough and ready,' he says, 'but they are good people. The best you'll get.' He has lived in Nitshill most of his adult life, brought his children up here and is saddened at what some of the younger inhabitants get up to.

The week before there had been a robbery involving both violence and thousands of pounds. The week before that the police had come into the bar and searched everybody. Of course, drugs are a problem in the area although it is unusual for pubs ever to be used as market-places – deserted housing is the favoured spot – social areas are where pushers can often be found. There was no evidence at all that The Royal Oak harboured any of the pushers. The bar is clean and well-cared for, with no slash marks in the plastic seating and no cigarette burns on the carpets, and the customers talk energetically and warmly to each other. A decent community with too much trouble around it.

There is not much prosperity in Nitshill and little in Pollok either. There is a lavish, covered shopping centre in the latter spot and people come from miles around to make their purchases. The sad fact is that the locals are unlikely to be able to afford much of what goes on sale in the very heart of the district in which they live. The people here are poor. A huge number of the children – more than half – come from single-parent families.

Everywhere you go in the schemes you will come across these single-parent families. Divorce, separation, more often than not common-law husbands who just piss off, tired of the economic struggle and the consequent emotional difficulties which people of poor education and low cultural expectations seem to adopt as some kind of bulwark against a societal conformity. Increasingly the young women, some as young as fifteen and sixteen, get pregnant intentionally, even vindictively, against society. It gives these teenagers a role in life rather than passive unemployment and they get houses, often sub-standard, from the Council, but at least they can move away from their nagging mums who have had to put up with the same kind of privation, having been single parents themselves.

In many of the areas like Nitshill or Pollok (or in the North, Drumchapel and Blackhill and elsewhere), the insistent hopelessness is compounded by the nature of lumpen proletarian culture. Nobody much cares, least of all the lumpen themselves. There is a self-perpetuity as complex as that enjoyed by the upper classes: a kind of inverted *Forsyte Saga*. Areas like this, all over the other Glasgow, have societal breakdown cast over them like a miasma of locusts, eating into the fabric of the lives therein. Doctors telephone the police to find out if addresses are valid before they go out on home visits, because of the ever-present problem of muggings by drug addicts. Some of the streets are no-go areas for the police anyway, though the police will officially deny this. Firemen get stoned by the locals when they arrive to put out fires. Glasgow has the highest number of fire-related fatalities in the world outside of Soweto and that township enjoys the advantage in the fire figures because of the 'necklace' murders. Huge areas of the 'Glasgow of the Schemes' could be Soweto itself.

Contrary to the popular imagination of the rest of the UK and beyond, Glasgow possesses a large and flourishing bourgeoisie and always has. For there is another Glasgow as well as the drab housing estates. Not far from the Nitshills and Polloks is Pollokshields. Here you will find stone-built mansions which would go for two or three million in London, big fine houses, testaments to Edwardian confidence and complacency. Many of them now house retirement or children's homes. Of those that house actual families, one has to ask how it can be done: what level of income can possibly support such splendour.

New money is here too, as represented by the ranch-style houses preferred by the *nouveau riche* – property developers, businessmen in the motor trade, highly paid football players. Celtic manager Billy McNeill once stayed in just such a house in this area. Outside one of the later houses are six cars in the drive. Two are Mercedes. One is a Roller. The exclusive Haggs Castle Golf Club is nearby. Local Craigholme School can accommodate the daughters of the natives, if they can pay for the privilege that is. The Craigholme girls wear a school uniform elaborate enough for the Household Cavalry and carry lacrosse nets with them besides their empty briefcases.

The big houses are set in leafy lanes, ideal for raising a quiet and douce bourgeoisie. Seconds away, across the Shields Road, there are the teeming tenements of the once genteel lower middle classes, now a huddle of Asian, mainly Pakistani, families. Not an inconsiderable number of the same one-time immigrant families are moving inexorably into the old Pollokshields. This has not brought down house prices. If you can afford to move into the Edwardian palaces you will be readily accepted. One thing ties districts of such wealth to schemes like Pollok not far away: there is almost no social focus at all. Pollokshields has no pubs, shops, restaurants, or anything else likely to bind a community together as you will find in the older, tenemental districts. Here, as in all the dormitory-style housing schemes, decent people roll the boulder in front of the cave when they get home at night.

A few miles away you can find Newlands which will mirror the same quiet and settled luxury. Across the Clyde there is Kelvinside. Cheek by jowl with slum areas too. There is, surprisingly, little class conflict in Glasgow though there is certainly an economic barrier. Few Glaswegians utter in the Anglo-Scots tones that you will find separating the classes in other cities in the UK. You will not find the deference between the lower and the upper orders which is prevalent in, say, Edinburgh. There is a communality in the pubs for a start and democracy is never far away from the Glasgow consciousness.

These are the other Glasgows, and there are more too. Cathcart, which thinks of itself as a contained village. Carmunnock, which *is* a village complete with a bucolic peasantry. Baillieston which thrives but claims itself immunity from the rest of the East End of Glasgow. They are all a far cry from what the modern Glasgow is seen to represent. Maryhill, on the north side, a long-established working-class district, has been refurbished to the point at which it must be one of the best housing developments in the entire country, and possesses a community profile strong enough to be a major force in the city.

Not all of Glasgow – not much of it really – will be the City of Culture. Yet Glasgow was the first city to re-invent itself after the devastation of the slum clearance years and their aftermath. It may very well be found to have been the most successful and the most imaginative city in that endeavour. Still the peripheral schemes, like the bleak estates which ring all British cities, will show, for a long time, another need besides culture and confidence. And the sedate laagers of the discrete bourgeoisie will, as they have always done, largely ignore both need and culture. For there is confidence and conflict and despair within those parts which all the arts cannot reach.

JACK WEBSTER

The Media

AS SCOTLAND'S LARGEST AND BUSIEST CITY, GLASGOW WAS ALWAYS DESTINED
to be the centre of the nation's newspaper, radio and television activity; and
so it has been down the years, from the days of hot metal in the newspaper
printing trade through to the age of electronic news-gathering, direct-input
and so much else which comes to bewilder us in this madly modern
world. Apart from producing most newspapers, it houses the Scottish
headquarters of the BBC and the country's largest independent station,
Scottish Television, in addition to Radio Clyde and Clyde Cablevision.
Nowadays such a collection has come to be known as 'the media', one of
those glib plurals, like 'criteria', which seem to induce a feeling of well-being
in the human race even when their meaning is little understood.

Everyone, however, understands the importance of the component parts
as they affect their daily lives, from catching a news bulletin on radio or
television to absorbing the fuller explanations in the morning or evening
newspaper. It takes only the rarity of a non-publication day to bring
forth the gasping reaction of the smoker deprived of a puff. From the
weightier news and features to the football stories, racing tips, crossword
or horoscope, there is an insatiable appetite for the printed word. In short,
the people need their newspapers and, in varying permutations of title, style
and taste, the Scottish public have had them in abundance throughout this
century. While Edinburgh, Dundee and Aberdeen have each been served
by a morning and evening paper, Glasgow could parade, in one particular
period, its *Glasgow Herald, Bulletin* and *Evening Times, Daily Record,
Evening News* and *Sunday Mail, Scottish Daily Express, Evening Citizen*
and *Scottish Sunday Express*, with a major share of other publications,
like D.C. Thomson's *Sunday Post*. The arrival of television in time for
the Queen's Coronation of 1953 began to change public perceptions and
it soon became apparent that a city like Glasgow, for example, could
not sustain three evening papers. The *News* dropped out. Likewise, the
Herald's stable-mate, the *Bulletin*, and later the *Citizen*, ceased publication.
The revolution has been turning ever since, bringing a whole new way of
producing papers which is much more cost-effective and labour-saving.

Although that revolution had already started when I arrived in Glasgow,
in the opening days of the sixties, the mood of journalism at that time
was still fairly heavily rooted in the pre-war period of belted raincoats and
soft felt hats. It may even have been that Humphrey Bogart image which
turned the mind of many a youngster like myself to thoughts of journalism
as a career. From the unvarnished life of rural Scotland, it seemed like the
distant promise of glamour, epitomised by the name of Fleet Street. Having
taken the preliminary route through local newspapers, I set my starry eyes
on Glasgow and can still rekindle the inner acceleration which took me up
the staircase of that glass palace in Albion Street, which is now the home
of the *Glasgow Herald* and *Evening Times* but was then the Scottish base
of Lord Beaverbrook's *Express*.

The Press barons had ruled supreme throughout the great era of journal-

The Evening
Times *proclaims
the outbreak of
war, 1939.*

The old Glasgow Herald *building.*

ism. Essentially they were journalists themselves, in retrospect, men with a genuine passion for the profession as opposed to a later breed which seemed more concerned with profit than professional pride. There were some remarkable stories, like that of the Berry family from Wales, a single household which produced sons William, who became Lord Camrose, Henry, who became Lord Buckland, and Gomer, Lord Kemsley, all newspaper barons owning more than a hundred national and provincial publications between them. Lord Kemsley's vast empire included his Glasgow group of *Record, News* and *Sunday Mail*, based in Hope Street, opposite the Central Hotel, with a large picture window which displayed the whole printing process to a public still fascinated by such spectacles. Across in Albion Street, running down from George Street to Ingram Street, Lord Beaverbrook had come searching for a place to build a Scottish base in the twenties. He was the Scots-Canadian who had come back to the land of his fathers, taken over the London *Daily Express* at the end of the First World War, turned it into the most widely read daily newspaper in the world – but wouldn't rest until he had established a Scottish *Express* as well. That happened in Albion Street, Glasgow, in 1928, when he converted an old tobacco factory and created that same black-glass frontage which survives to this day.

It was into the bustle of that building that I stepped on Leap Year Night, 1960, to become a sub-editor on the *Scottish Daily Express*, a paper which was building towards a daily sale of 640,000 copies, at that time the highest figure achieved by any Scottish daily. Life for the reporter was still a pretty feverish pursuit of news, the patterns of which seem to have changed over the years. Glasgow was still playing out a longstanding tradition of gangs, razor-slashing and protection rackets, while capable of producing the occasional colourful character, like Johnny Ramensky, the notorious safe-blower who was parachuted in to blow enemy safes during the Second World War before returning to his own more personal enterprises, which gave him a high residential qualification within the stark walls of Peterhead Prison.

In more sinister fashion, the murder trial of Peter Manuel, Scotland's most notorious mass killer, had just come to an end with the hangman's noose when I took up residence in the Burnside district of the city where Manuel had murdered the family of a prominent baker, William Watt. Sub-editors, walking home in the early hours to clear the head of a smoke-filled night, would go in twos or threes for safety. Behind them lay sub-editing tables bestrewn with scraps of unwanted copy, scissors, glue-pots, cigarette ends and tea-stained cups, the lull after the night storm in which the *Record* and *Express* would battle it out for readers, recording late-night life in Glasgow, from the sophisticated to the seedy, until the very last minute of possible publication. Meanwhile, across in Mitchell Street, the *Glasgow Herald* went its own less frenetic way, cherishing a readership of a different sort and perhaps regarding itself as being above that unseemly scramble for sales.

Ironically, it was in that sixties period of unprecedented affluence that the seeds of destruction for the all-conquering *Scottish Daily Express* were sown. Attempts by the management to correct what they regarded as over-staffing met with such a ferocity of union opposition from the journalists as would be hard to understand in 1990. With a high level of political motivation, it has to be said, the situation deteriorated to a point where, between March 1973 and March 1974, they stopped the paper completely on sixteen occasions and interrupted production on fifty-six more nights. Given the perishable nature of newspapers, there was, of course, no way in which that situation could continue. For whatever reason, a dominant knot of militants failed to heed warnings that the paper would close and, in an atmosphere which they alleged was positively intimidating, the silent majority stayed silent too long. In March 1974, Beaverbrook Newspapers announced it was ceasing the Glasgow publication of the *Scottish Daily Express, Evening Citizen* and *Scottish Sunday Express* and would serve Lord Beaverbrook's beloved nation from Manchester instead. Few could have been surprised. Around 1,800 people were made redundant in what was perhaps the most dramatic development in the story of Scottish newspapers.

In a period of upswing for Scottish nationalism, Beaverbrook was lambasted for its move to England. It was all good, sloganeering stuff and, for all the power of the Press, it found itself unable to convince the Scottish people that it had been more sinned against than sinning. Operating from the distance of Manchester, the *Express* sales slumped, understandably, and the popular daily paper field north of the border was left to the *Record*, which landed a near monopoly. Any editor who could fail to carry the paper to new levels of circulation in that situation would have been thoroughly deserving of the sack.

Meanwhile, back at Albion Street, the cherished dream of some militants – to run their own newspaper, as it turned out – was assisted by Beaverbrook no less, who co-operated in letting them have the former *Express* plant. With his socialist declarations, the fastly-emerging Robert Maxwell was also pitching in with a personal presence of support. The workers' co-operative would run its own *Scottish Daily News*, in which the redundant could invest their money. Some gave more than others (and claimed they were astounded how little some others had given!) but the bottom line of this sorry saga was that, while working twice as hard for less money, they all went down the publishing plughole, having discovered that running a newspaper at that particular period was not so simple as they had hoped.

Some who helped to fashion the *Scottish Daily News* perished in a winter of their own discontent and the course of newspaper history in this country began to change. With the advent of Thatcherism in 1979 and the neutering of union leaders like Arthur Scargill, there have been consequences for journalists and others which show how far the pendulum has swung in favour of employers. Would it be unreasonable to pose the question of how far that would have been necessary if people like the Beaverbrook journalists of the late sixties and early seventies had counted their good fortune and kept an even keel?

By then empty and deserted, in ghostly contrast to that zenith in Scotland's newspaper history, Albion Street was taken over by the elder statesman of the nation's Press, the George Outram organisation, in need of more room than was available in the old Mitchell Street premises, behind Buchanan Street. So the *Glasgow Herald* and *Evening Times* moved in among the Beaverbrook ghosts in 1979 and began their own rise to new levels of ambition and success. Like most other newspaper organisations, of course, they were still stuck with a technology which was hopelessly out of date. Intransigent attitudes emanating from Fleet Street print unions, naturally protecting their own interests, were hampering progress from what everyone knew was a ridiculously cumbersome process. It was known as 'hot metal', in which every line of type was cast into a slug of lead which was built to last for generations. Yet, as soon as it had passed its imprint to that virgin page of the night, it was promptly melted down, skimmed, cleansed and restored for the next day's paper.

Revolutionary new methods were waiting in the wings while management

A crowd gathers to watch Scotland's first official British television broadcast, 1952.

A Scottish Daily News demonstration, 1975.

and unions assumed their respective stances. It took an English provincial newspaper owner, Mr Eddy Shah, to face the inevitable hostility and break the mould of outdated practice. Having prised open the door, he made it easier for Rupert Murdoch to repeat the performance at national level, taking his prestigious *Times* of London through stormy waters to a new, computerised home at Wapping, albeit with much violence on the way. Yet who can argue about the wisdom of the change? The day of the video display unit had arrived, with journalists keying in their own copy and rendering the hot metal brigade of type-setters largely superfluous. The cost of producing newspapers was substantially reduced and everybody was bound to benefit. By the mid-eighties the Glasgow papers were free to move towards the new technologies.

Earlier in that decade, Outram had embarked on an ambitious project to produce a Glasgow-based quality Sunday paper, the *Sunday Standard*. Launched in 1981, with a recession hovering, the paper ran into losses which were not sustainable and was finally closed in July 1983, a short-lived venture which nevertheless fired the imagination of the Scottish people, who appreciated the fact that they had, at last, a Sunday paper of their own which could take its place among the best from London. In the improved climate of a few years later, the *Sunday Standard* might well have survived to become one of the more profitable weekend journals; but it was not to be.

By the late eighties, the *Glasgow Herald* and *Evening Times* were benefiting from a £22 million investment in the latest printing and inserting technology, which included colour (a development in which the *Daily Record* had led the field among British dailies). By now the *Record* was in the ownership of Mirror Newspapers, which meant the irrepressible Robert Maxwell, already free of competition from the *Scottish Daily Express* and not much the better for that. Inasmuch as competition is the lifeblood of newspapers, there was a glaring need for someone to challenge them in their tabloid field, though the appearance of a serious rival seemed unlikely. However, the new technologies enabled Rupert Murdoch's organisation, with all the modern facsimile techniques, to start printing the *Sun* (as well as the *Times* of London) at a plant in Kinning Park, just across the Clyde from the *Record* building at Anderston Quay, which had replaced the old Hope Street base. The battle for readership rages into the nineties. Neither, of course, has a Scottish owner, though Murdoch has the edge on local claims over the Czechoslovakian-born Maxwell, his grandfather having been minister at Hatton of Cruden, near Peterhead, before the whole Murdoch family emigrated from Aberdeenshire to Australia two generations ago. Tabloid warfare produced some pretty unsavoury results in the eighties but we return to the old axiom which says that, as with governments, a society gets the newspapers it deserves. If people didn't buy them, they would not survive.

Meanwhile, radio and television continue to play their own significant part in the life of Glasgow and Scotland, largely unaffected by the kind of drastic changes which can beset their printed counterparts. The BBC provides Scotland's widest radio and television service from its headquarters at Queen Margaret Drive. Scottish Television opened its doors in 1957 when another of the Commonwealth entrepreneurs, Mr Roy Thomson, was granted the franchise for commercial television in central Scotland. It was then, with his prior experience of this medium in North America, that Mr Thomson made his remark about having been granted a licence to print money. It is a comment which haunted him and his successors ever after, though there were uncertain periods when advertising revenues dropped. Profits did rise, however, to £9 million in 1989, on a turnover of £92 million, compared to £2 million ten years earlier. The original home at the Theatre Royal was later replaced by a new building next door.

In commercial broadcasting, Radio Clyde has been an unqualified success, a kind of flagship which soon dispelled doubts which lingered over the viability of the medium, as a result of early hiccups with the London stations. Its many innovations included the introduction of a twenty-four-hour news room and it now owns North Sound Radio in Aberdeen. Clyde's first home was at the Anderston Centre, just above the bus station, where it first broadcast on Hogmanay night, 1973. Ten years later it moved to new premises at Clydebank, on the site of the old Singer sewing machine factory.

Side by side with the Press, radio and television, their life-supporting industry of advertising has been making its own stridies, symbolised perhaps by the appaearance and success of the magazine *Scotmedia*, which the agencies have come to regard as their own. Statistics are hard to come by but, in *Scotmedia*'s Premier Division of agencies, six of the twelve Scottish leaders are based in Glasgow and had billings of £74 million in 1989. They included well-known names like Rex Stewart, Struthers, Charles Barker, Ogilvy and Mather, Craig and Grant Forrest.

Public relations has also been growing along parallel lines. In 1980, there were eight companies trading as public relations consultants in Glasgow, employing around 200 to 250 people. Ten years later, there are more than twenty consultancies and, with the growth of in-house services, it is an industry now.

Publishing has always leaned more towards Edinburgh than Glasgow, though the latter could claim one of the giants of the industry, William Collins and Sons, founded in 1819. Based for many years at its Cathedral Street headquarters, Collins became well known as world-wide printers of the Bible. While editorial control rests in London, much of the Collins printing and distribution operation still takes place at Bishopbriggs, where there are 1600 employees.

Among the smaller Glasgow publishers, Richard Drew has gained prominence in the 1980s, having taken over the former Molendinar Press and caught the eye of the reading public with his distinctive bookshop displays of the Scottish Collection. Glasgow subjects figure largely in his list, along with the reprints of popular Scottish titles.

So Glasgow embraces the largest share of media expression in Scotland. Despite longstanding cries about a Tory Press in Britain, the balance of newspaper support in Scotland in this latter part of the twentieth century could be said to have leaned more and more towards socialism and nationalism, partly reflecting public opinion as well as helping to form it.

From the point of view of the journalist, newspaper life is a much less frenetic business than it used to be. With the smell of printer's ink, glue-pots and molten lead gone, with the clack of the typewriter now regarded as a noisy intrusion, the atmosphere of an editorial floor has become one of carpeted calm, hushed tones and quiet computers – an almost sinister silence. Maybe it can be argued that people think better that way. Just permit an old hack the thought that noise and bustle in that mid-century madness released the adrenaline, generated a fiery enthusiasm and helped to produce great newspapers. While pursuing the facts, you could tighten that raincoat belt, tilt the soft felt hat and swagger off with a hint of Hollywood in your hips. Like life itself, I believe, journalism works better when you are having fun!

ROBERT McLAUGHLAN

Drinking in Glasgow

DRINKING IN GLASGOW HAS BEEN TRANSFORMED SINCE THE END OF THE
Second World War. That event in itself did not change too much but the
advent of mass travel in the late fifties and sixties and the emancipation
of women certainly did. The years of austerity which characterised the war
and its immediate aftermath handed on an earlier pattern of hard drinking,
overwhelmingly male, in which cheap grain or blended whisky was used to
'chase' pints of sweet, heavy beer.

All but the 'dry', *petit bourgeois*, areas of the city were festooned with
pubs – even smallish streets in working-class areas usually boasted several –
and these were the main venues for consumption. Although some provision
was made for women, it was marginal – neither the environments nor
the kinds of drink the pubs offered had much appeal for young single
women, nor indeed their married counterparts. (Courting couples did not
patronise pubs.) Sawdust floors were obligatory when fairly widespread
spitting added to the problems of spillage. Toilet facilities were poor – for
women, often non-existent – and although the fittings and decor in some
particular cases were splendid enough to be preserved today, and even
copied by contemporary 'theme' pubs, the generality was uninviting.

It would be wrong to assume that women did not participate in pub life
at all for some pubs did have a female clientèle, but it was usually small.
Some few pubs had 'family' departments where ladies, or husbands and
wives, could sit and drink separately from the main shop; but the 'family'
was usually a euphemism for a tiny room which operated for 'off' sales.
Women were mostly expected to drink at home to where draught beer
was often taken in large jugs, and spirits in a variety of small bottles,
mostly smaller than the present half-bottle. Actually the male-dominated
society sought to segregate drinking sexually – and even frowned on female
drinking to the extent that some women who wanted to drink regularly
often had to affect a commitment to 'tonics' consumed in the home. These
were usually cheap fortified wines (often called 'burgundy') or port. Port
was considered a respectable working-class drink – but wine was not. This
unfavourable social image was a major drawback to the first hard mass
marketing of table wines in the late sixties and seventies.

There was another segment of the market – that in fine wines and spirits.
It was small. The city had a goodly spread of licensed grocers but not many
boasted a significant range of fine wines. The best known exception was
Ferguson's of Union Street which did have a good selection of fine wines,
particularly white Burgundies and sweet whites. Of specialist fine wine
merchants of quality, Sandeman's of West George Street was certainly
well stocked with vintage ports and clarets including the Premiers Crus,
(I owe all my first experiences of Mouton Rothschild to purchases there
in the early sixties) but the backbone of the business was understandably
less exalted.

Of restaurants with fine wine lists there were few as well. The Malmaison
in the Central Hotel was legendary – and expensive. Ferrari's, then at the

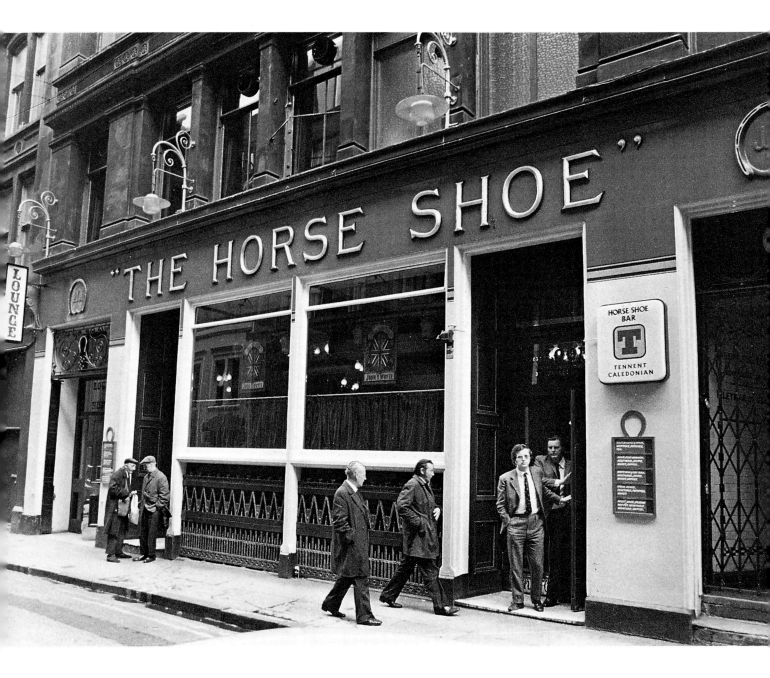

A Glasgow hotel
bar, 1962.

Charing Cross end of Sauchiehall Street, was a more reasonably priced alternative, but the overall selection was restricted. This began to change slowly but the pace picked up as several influences reinforced each other. The creation of the vast peripheral housing schemes all completely devoid of pubs through the deliberate policy of a council dominated by the anti-drink lobby, forced the drinks industry to construct new outlets on the nearest edges of permitted licensed districts. These were large, and therefore costly: most were owned by the brewing companies. They needed to be far more attractive than their predecessors since customers could not drop in so casually as before but had to travel a bit – for example they were lavishly carpeted and had well-upholstered seating, especially in their 'lounges' (the sure sign of a female clientèle for whom they had adequate lavatory facilities).

These new pubs marked a break with the hard-drinking male culture and their significance is bound to be noticed by future social historians who will also connect the changes with the beginnings of the lager boom and the move to lighter beers. Social investigators may also seize upon the importance of mass foreign holiday travel in familiarising millions of ordinary people, when abroad, with beverages thought to be suspect at home. Cheap fortified wine – Lanliq, Eldorado, Three Crowns – all in fact the same thing under different flags – was consumed in great quantity but enjoyed no 'ton'; quite the reverse. Foreign holidays changed that, not for the fortified stuff, now often known as British wine, but for ordinary wines. Cheap but sound unfortified wine, sipped under a hot sun and with local cuisine creating the taste by which it was to be enjoyed.

The rise of the supermarket chains coincided with this movement – and went on to supply cheap wine nationally over the last two or three decades, their huge buying power keeping prices low. It is more than ten years since the Scottish Co-operative Wholesale Society found more Scots saying they drank wine rather than whisky. The Co-operators were slower into the wine business themselves since they had been part of the Scottish anti-drink movement (which actually elected the only Prohibitionist in British parliamentary history, though not in Glasgow). But even the Co-op changed, and now sells wine as well as anyone else.

These are national trends, but are everywhere mirrored here; it is impossible in drink to identify a distinct Scottish culture though some regional sub-cultures undoubtedly exist, for example in rum consumption which is well documented. The main trend now is to white wine of progressively drier kinds. Glaswegians have a legendary sweet tooth (a heritage of the West Indian sugar trade to Clydeside) and were prone to dilute their whisky with sweet lemonade or accompany their early curries with lashings of sweet Spanish 'Chablis' or Spanish 'Sauternes' (sic!). It may still be the case that drinkers prefer their wines to be sweeter in the mouth than on the label but the consumption of uncompromisingly dry Sauvignons from Touraine, Bordeaux, New Zealand and California, and the new light dry Italians from the Tyrol is growing fast in Glasgow. This will delight wine amateurs but it has to be added that the demand for cheap Niersteiner Gutes Domtal, Piesporter and Liebfraumilch is still strong enough to leave the image of all German wines dented.

Only Oddbins now comes near to stocking more than a few German wines of quality; only the Ubiquitous Chip restaurant near the University lists more than ten, although some hotels within striking distance of the city – the Crinan Hotel on the Sound of Jura and the Braeval Mill at Aberfoyle – offer a few quality trocken wines. The first has a Schloss

Vollrads Halbtrocken, for example, the second a fine Franken trocken among others in the same style. Lafite's, a Chinese restaurant at the even nearer new town of East Kilbride, boasts some, as well as several more traditional Germans good enough to enthuse about.

Glasgow has a vibrant Italian community which sells its wines mainly through restaurants. The mark-up on these invites the same sort of gripe to which wine-lovers are prone everywhere and one result is that it really is rare to encounter the magical best Italians like Sassicaia (but try La Parmigiana in the city's Great Western Road) or old Piedmontese (though La Lanterna in Hope Street has some – at a price!) Some of the finer wines, however, are often stocked by the likes of Fazzi Brothers in both Cambridge Street and Clyde Street. Even the supermarket chains are beginning to display some Italian equivalents of the good French reds they sell – Marks and Spencer is an example. A quick generalisation would remain: the glories of Italian wine are obscure in the West of Scotland. Edinburgh is far better placed.

The city is still short of independent wine merchants. Two recent attempts to establish wholesale traders – selling by the case – failed. One new creation of the last few years, Peckhams, with three branches, seems to be flourishing. Of chains, Peter Dominic is sadly poorly represented (it came and went from the city centre rather quickly) but Victoria Wine, which also owns Haddows, sometimes seems to be everywhere. Most of its branches, however, stock only the cheaper end of its remarkable range dominated by East European wines, particularly Bulgarian reds (excellent value for money) and Yugoslavian whites. Only odd branches, like that in nearby Milngavie, show what a Victoria Wine list can be like when visible on the shelves.

Oddbins is therefore left in a class by itself. It has a clutch of shops and two are particularly well-placed to tap the West End market around the University. It has well-trained staff who can offer sound opinions on many of the items in stock. Each branch seems to have the whole range which is particularly rich in American (not just Californian) and antipodean wines. Oddbins too holds the best range of fine French wines, though it is better on Bordeaux than Burgundy. It seems, too, to do well in spirits with an interesting clutch of fine malt whiskies, cognacs, armagnacs and even more *recherché* items.

The supermarket chains are here what they are everywhere, which is both a strength and a weakness. Tesco in Pollok can, however, claim to have one specialised line – because of the concentration of the city's Jewish community on the South side, this store has a wide selection of kosher wines as well as its normal range. Safeways has been trading up and invites attention for its modestly priced middle-ranking white Burgundies. Marks has its line of second wines from famous Bordeaux châteaux and seems to do very well from the city's recently acquired appetite for champagne (which has been large enough to excite the wonder of the Champagne Bureau).

Champagne is in fact widely available in almost every kind of restaurant of which Glasgow now has a very large number of new creations in addition to the Italian and 'ethnic' outlets. A common assumption seems to be that this drink requires pricing out of reach and reasonable restaurant prices are rare – for half bottles, only the Colonial in High Street and Fouquet's in Renfield Street spring to mind; for bottles only the Ubiquitous Chip near the University (strangely, in its case, since it has the best wine list in the city, the selection is rather short, with Pol Roger stealing the show). But no city restaurant list boasts more than a sprinkling of champagne entries, though the Crinan Hotel (an hour and a half's drive away) is intending to carry all

*Fazzi Brothers'
shop, 1989.*

sixteen Grands Marques to complement the long run of still whites in its sea-food restaurant.

The Ubiquitous Chip is the Mecca of local wine lovers and it has a separate wine shop where most of the items on a compendious list, which is strong in claret and Côtes du Rhone, are available at retail prices. The real attraction of this list is that it remains reasonably priced, especially for its choicest items – only the gourmet restaurants of rural Scotland seem to affect the same policy. There is no doubt that it acts as a magnet for the establishment which has a little additional trick of its own in a very long list of Scottish malt whiskies sold by the glass and offered in more generous measures than has been common of late.

Other restaurants have particular strengths. Triangle in Queen Street has some fine – and expensive – Alsace and some reasonable Loire wines. The Colonial has the Lebanon's Château Musar at an affordable price. It also is trying to build a long list and occasionally has old wines for well-off connoisseurs. The Buttery in Anderston has some decent Australian reds and indeed these and New Zealand whites are probably the best buys around since they are not inflated in price beyond their quality. They are a godsend to drinkers and a threat to the French whose wines often suffer from the sort of premium mark-up which seems to leave champagne sales unaffected.

Ethnic restaurants are mainly Indian and highly spiced curries are death to fine wines, with only the more aggressive Gewurztraminers being able to hold their own. The first of the post-war Indian restaurants was opened near the University in the late fifties. Since then they have proliferated. Most are wise to offer lager (but why do so few produce decent coffee when India exports the appealing Mysore?). Balbir's Indian Brasserie in Sauchiehall Street is the only one with a longish list containing some fine wines and India's own rather good sparkler, Omar Khayyam. The Thai restaurant in the same street, but further east, is on strong ground with its beer.

Sadly, Chinese restaurants are not strong on wine and China's own Great Wall should probably be avoided – it's too heavy and well maderised – but some of the Chinese are concentrating on French whites. The Peking Inn near the top of Hope Street is one such. Lafite's in East Kilbride is quite exceptional for its wines and well worth the travelling time.

Wines in pubs are, generally, not a success but they are sold everywhere, as they are in the cafés and wine bars which have multiplied even faster than restaurants. Neither of these last tends to have anything special except in the late autumn when the cult of Beaujolais Nouveau is celebrated with gusto and sometimes with the genuine pleasure which a good vintage can ensure from this otherwise slight wine. They do, however, sell enough sound cheap wine to the extent that Glasgow's is no longer a hard-drinking culture.

All of these are forces which have helped to end any sexual segregation in drinking. The result must sound like the Yuppie culture, and it is true that wine drinkers tend to be younger rather than older but too much should not be made of this. Every age and social class has been affected by wine. It may be that its arrival has not so much squeezed competitors out as greatly expanded the market for alcohol. There seems to be much more drunk now than ever before. That is true of beer as well, though the city has not been fast, or much, into the real ale movement. The Bon Accord near Charing Cross, however, has long made a specialty of traditionally brewed beers. A recent change of ownership has reduced its appeal in this respect but Mitchell's nearby is an alternative stocking several real ales including Belhaven. The Victoria Bar near the Briggait and the Mitre in Brunswick Street are also to be recommended in this context. The Boswell Hotel and Country Club in the southside's Mansion House Road is a step ahead still in that it always has at least six real ales on hand pump, and its list changes weekly.

Tennent's lager remains the best selling lager in and around Glasgow but many younger drinkers have gone heavily into imported foreign beers like Grolsch from Holland and Furstenburg from Germany. These are widely available in draught or bottle; but a remarkable range of other imported beers from as far afield as the West Indies and Japan are available in and drunk directly from their cans. These products are often relatively high in alcohol and always expensive. Perhaps the point most worth making in this context is that beer has ceased to be a cheap drink. Its position *vis-à-vis* whisky has been reversed, a fact which may be obscured by the way in which the finer malt whiskies have succeeded in marketing themselves at prices much higher than the old established proprietary blends let alone their even poorer competitors.

Whisky may have been squeezed by vodka and light white rums (dark rums have certainly been a casualty, along with sherry) but marketing successes have arrested a trend. Not just in the case of malts where specialist pubs have actually appeared to boost these (The Pot Still in Hope Street and the Maltman in its parallel Renfield Street). The growth in sales of Famous Grouse shows that clever marketing of a sound product can create a new, and profitable, customer base. Others are trying hard to follow this lead.

What stands out is the variety of alcoholic experience now available. The global village has arrived in Glasgow. Some things have gone, including much of the tradition of singing in pubs, last remnant of the West Highland (and Irish?) popular cultures. Not all the loss evokes sadness: for all that we drink much more collectively we seem to drink with more caution individually, and drunkenness is not what it was, at least not in public.

*The distinctive
Mackintosh front
at Henderson's
shop, 1981.*

ANNE SIMPSON

Glasgow Style

NOW THIS MAY SURPRISE YOU. WHILE THE ENGLISH BUSINESSMAN ABROAD IS still too often identified by a certain seedy fatigue about the waistline, the Scotsman, or more specifically the Glaswegian, emerges, in any pinstripe throng, as elegant and taut, the owner of twenty shirts in fashionable working order, the possessor of a fine gold chain around his neck and on his wrist, most probably, a Rolex denoting upward mobility in circles highly serious about time. These are not the ramblings of a deranged fashion writer but the findings of various solid market research studies carried out over recent years on behalf of the British menswear industry. At its most detailed such data reveals not just the Glaswegian's superiority in the matter of shirt tails – the average man here owns more than his equivalent brother anywhere else in Britain – but also the sparkling role ornamentation plays in his life. No matter how discreet, his cuff-links are meant to be observed.

Glasgow, of course, has always dealt brazenly in superlatives, sending shivers of disapproval down Edinburgh's prim spine. Yet one leading jeweller with outlets in both cities once disclosed that he lost more items through theft in the capital than he did forty miles away in the west. In general he suffered one break-in a month in Glasgow while in Edinburgh some costly bauble was lifted almost every week by professional gangs up from the South whose ultimate refinement was the elderly fur-coated lady acting as a decoy. In Glasgow the raw ebullience of smash-'n'-grab prevailed. But while Edinburgh men disguise what they spend on clothes by sheltering in the safe traditionalism of tweeds and sober suits, Glasgow men listen to the language of fashion, its code of status signals, and rapidly respond. Does all this prancing around, this looking sharp in the definitive leather blouson or the draped Numero Uno jacket suggest that effetism is now sweetening Glasgow's macho armpit? Who can be sure? But much has changed utterly and much has to do with a new attitude of mind which doesn't ask men to become dandies but requires that they be less repressed about sensuality and self-expression.

Among Glasgow's daughters, of course, visual panache has always been the thing. Long before the city's present remarkable revival, Recession Chic cohabited here quite naturally with multiple deprivation. By cultivating a strong, personal style, Glasgow women defied their turf's ugly reputation. Keeping up appearances welded body and soul together and thus the city of the hard shoulder became the city of the fast turnover, one of the first centres in Britain to sustain two mobbed Marks and Spencers, two bustling C & A's. So this battered old place became the rag trade's lingering *amour*, meticulously coiffed and enamelled, ready to strut through the dark with all the beckoning relish of sin. The other night a raven-haired girl in a white silk romper suit and black stockings was seen running for a Springburn bus. Scoffing chips from a poke, she appeared like some wild alliance between Theda Bara and a kindergarten. Where had she been, this self-regarding *ingénue*? Fury Murry's . . . the Sub Club . . . shaping about with her pals in all that pagan House music, practising her panda-eyed gaze and desire to look silently profound?

Today new money seeks the pedigree of international labels from The Warehouse, Ichi Ni San and Princes Square. Mappin and Webb in Glasgow sell a Rolex at around £2,000 practically every day of the week. Sax is the only shop in Scotland to stock Romeo Gigli and through the adventurous buying spirit of David Mullane at The Warehouse, Jean-Paul Gaultier, the most anarchic designer in Paris, can claim to have a Scottish chapter in the Merchant City.

Much tested in resilience, Glasgow's earthiness is never likely to allow *poseurs* to gain the upper hand. Even so one already detects certain little *arriviste* snobberies, a sniffy suspicion that in fashion (as in the general arts) the only good things are those that are imported. This is the reverse of that tedious London myopia about anything north of NW1 and equally as ill-founded. In fact it does nothing except mark out the truly provincial but more seriously it also puts at risk the very creative possibilities of those indigenous designers whose talent requires sustained investment rather than the smug tokenism of ineffectual start-up grants.

So, out of all the effervescent defiance that has bred a new Glasgow style, this latest generation of artists and fashion makers still learns the brutal way that Big Business in this country – unlike that in Italy, America, Germany and Japan – simply doesn't take risks with unknowns and innovation. Thus, on a shoestring and by favourable words of mouth, a handful of fashion designers – Lex McFadyen at the Cook Street Studios, Spencer Railton in the basement of his home, and Diana Cook of Sidewalk in the Virginia Galleries – spunkily work against the mainstream of style to prove that demand does exist here for clothes with idiosyncratic dash. Their aim is not necessarily to be shocking but to be small and different and notably good. But as they explain the struggles of their valiant careers, the limitations of Glasgow's revival as a manufacturing pivot are essentially defined.

This remains a deprived city bravely making the best of it, but its old heritage of highly skilled workers in precision industries has been lost. Inevitably, then, independent designers, whose work is the antithesis of mass production, find it depressingly difficult to locate manufacturers who are both keen on specialised production and capable of producing it in small quantities which, by their superior finish, will compare admirably with European equivalents.

For many the very first problem begins with the purchase of cloth. Mills and textile agents both in Scotland and England are simply indifferent to the needs of designers who only wish to buy 500 metres of fabric rather than 35,000 for, say, a capsule collection of high fashion shirts. Quite often this negative response is rooted in those old enemies of the imagination, complacency and indolence masquerading as caution; hindrances which have bedevilled many leading British designers forcing them to order their materials from abroad. In the past ten years the most adventurous of the Scottish mills, like Claridge, and Heather Mills, at Selkirk, have built their reputation on meeting the designer challenge, but their products remain out of reach to under-capitalised newcomers, no matter how sure their promise.

WASP, the artists' co-operative in Glasgow, is one enterprise which works to alert the market to the creative verve on its own patch, and in the refurbished railway arches of its Cook Street premises you will find the fashion designer Lex McFadyen, and Claire Heminsley, graphics artist of Incahoots, who share an address at Studio One. Lex, whose

Spencer Railton,
Glasgow fashion
designer.

Aly McAnloy,
printed textile
designer.

Incahoots in their
Glasgow studio.

interestingly detailed clothes evoke Gaultier in his more gentle moods, is one of those designers whose originality is assured but the absence of wide patronage makes his label elusive. Even so, he commands a loyal following among the art-grad *cognoscenti*. McFadyen, himself a graduate of Glasgow School of Art where he studied sculpture and mixed media, knows from his life-drawing classes precisely how the body moves – which is more than can be said for some of those now being cheered internationally as couturiers. 'The thing I hate is this obsession with one label only and the wearing of it as an élitist badge,' he says. 'Fashion becomes corrupted when that happens.' McFadyen also loathes the price hype associated with many designer clothes and aims as far as possible to keep his exclusive work in the region of £200 for jackets and £60 to £100 for skirts.

Like Claire Heminsley, he is both excited and wary about Glasgow's rebirth as Style City. 'What is happening is marvellous so long as it doesn't make the place effete. At all levels Glasgow now needs to do things really well and not just settle for putting a glossy lid on all the old deprivation.' Heminsley, who studied woven and embroidered textiles at Glasgow School of Art, is mainly known for her Mayfest posters and the firecracker dazzle of her Incahoots T-shirts, plus a small, intricate array of earrings, Arabic in style, and made of cut leather appliquéed with silk, overstitched with embroidery. Now however, with fellow designers, Jan Nimmo and Graven Images, she is concentrating on a range of printed furnishings and graphics for a consultant in London who will market them at home and abroad.

Much of Glasgow's European feel and its virile strength in the industrial arts is derived from the excellence and international standing of its Art School, designed by Scotland's master builder, Charles Rennie Mackintosh. Acknowledged by many architects today as one of the wonders of twentieth-century architecture, GSA continues to produce an impressive roll-call of designers, but it is an indication of Britain's lingering neglect of design that most are enticed to join the opposition, taking up significant appointments with some of the most challenging design teams overseas.

At the Glasgow Style offices, which aim to alert attention towards indigenous designers by promoting various exhibitions, Stephanie Roberts, the project co-ordinator, works with limited public funds to ease the double-bind that afflicts both the local artist and the artisan. 'The real problem is their initial lack of investment,' she says. 'This means they miss out on obtaining the marketing know-how which is vital today, and consequently however talented they may be, they simply can't expand.'

So, most creative individualists end up shelving the valiant notion of self-sufficiency, and work for somebody else. Dominic Snyder, whose powerful figurative jazz paintings illuminated the more bluesy and raunchy corners of Glasgow night life three or so years ago, is now preoccupied with graphics for Doges Designs, and Ian McDonald, one of the few people to develop innovative lighting, works for the BBC as a full-time set designer.

Of those who remain, Ronnie Bridges and Graven Images represent perhaps the most successful consultancies. Bridges, whose handsome elemental interior for Ichi Ni San provides the most sophisticated retail ambience in Scotland, is also the inspirational force behind the Glasgow Art Factory. He has designed the Trading Post decor and is presently involved with Mackintosh and Company, recreating some of Charles Rennie Mackintosh's work from the master's original drawings. His major venture for 1990 will involve turning the airy, ornamental space of the Briggait into an international night club complex for an English entertainments

Bangles of faceted plastic mosaics by Peter Chang, sculptor and jewellery maker.

Graven Images. Design team, left to right, Avril Proctor, Spencer Ball, Ross Hunter, Janice Kirkpatrick, Paul Gray, Gillian McInnes and Stuart Gilmore. Pictured in the attic of their Bath Street office.

Carol Smillie, model, 1989.

company. 'The fact is,' says Bridges, 'that for Scottish designers the really big commissions still come from outsiders who are rich and adventurous enough to guarantee you artistic freedom.'

Graven Images resolutely work to exterminate the cliché and avoid the modish whim. Ultimately it is the diverse talents of the company's three directors, Janice Fitzpatrick, Stuart Gilmour and Ross Hunter (two trained in graphics, the third in architecture) which make the concept work. But there is also a hard-headed realism that intelligent design shouldn't exclude the commercial. Yet while the studio-based graphics commissions comprise the outfit's main turnover, their bespoke furniture and lighting is made in Italy at a small manufacturing co-operative outside Salerno, which specialises in technical finesse. 'We simply haven't been able to find anyone in Britain who could produce innovative pieces to such an excellent finish and at competitive prices,' says Janice, 'although this is precisely the kind of manufacturing that Scotland especially should be about. The future for a small country has to lie with quality now.'

On the south side of the city Peter Chang, born and raised in Liverpool and now a resident in Glasgow, is one of the most excitingly original jewellery makers in Europe today. In Italy his work has been bought by the Missonis; in Holland it has been shown at the classy Gallerie Ra in Amsterdam; in London Britain's Designer of the Year, Rifat Ozbek, has used Chang's brilliant geegaw to accessorise his clothes. What is especially significant is that the jewellery contains no fabulous gems. Chang, a sculptor who studied first at Liverpool College of Art, then in Paris and finally at the Slade in London, scavenges for discarded plastics and, like an alchemist, transmutes them into items of value and desire. 'Plastic is anonymous. It only has the character you give it,' he says. 'And I have always liked its tactile quality.'

Earrings may sell at around £50 but a bangle may be close on £1,000 because it will have taken Chang almost fifty labour-intensive hours to create its mosaic, carving the shape from a polystyrene base, then building and faceting it with hundreds of tiny plastic pieces recycled from the usual debris of any household – worn-out toothbrushes, coat hangers, battered toys and redundant felt-tip pens. This is the exacting artistry of a perfectionist but Chang finds himself almost mocked by his own severe demands: if he continues to work with such intense and time-consuming commitment to every piece (four-hour stretches of concentration, wearing a protective mask against adhesive fumes, are his limit), he may never make the jewellery pay. The alternative would be to simplify its line, form and colour in preparation for mass production. But then, will it still be art? Chang has taken the tackiness out of plastic and replaced it with extravagant beauty. Like any maestro, he doesn't wish to retreat from that achievement.

It is a compliment to Glasgow, though, that so many of its designers wish to stay here, believing that as soon as proper financial backing can be found, the Big Time will be but one dream commission or catwalk show away. Aly McAuley, one of the most gifted of young printed textile designers in Britain today (and a former apprentice electrician with Yarrow shipbuilders) has just completed his post-graduate year at GSA and is in the process of establishing a workshop in the city where he can further develop his wondrously elaborate botanical designs which reflect the tight, explicit flower drawings of the eighteenth century.

To general regret, of course, GSA has no actual fashion faculty, yet it may be that it is this very absence of formal training which gives the city's fashion designers their sheer creative nerve. Certainly the lack of a fashion degree seems not to have hindered the irrepressible Spencer Railton whose tulle and sequin *raison d'etre* has found a pantingly appreciative audience over the past three years. He mocks his work as 'trash-fash' but redeems the Dallasty connotations by equipping it with satirical edge.

Many of Glasgow's stylists create their own *arrondissements*, west of the city mainly, between Kelvinbridge and Byres Road, or re-emerging around the merchant quarter to the east. But in all this flutter to proclaim Glasgow as designers' territory, one fact is still being overlooked: designers cannot live by creative drive alone. The wretched truth is that despite its stirring, we'll-do-better pledges, British industry remains uncommitted to exploiting design in any deep and lasting way. Individually Glaswegians with their shameless glitzkreig exuberance will always know how to dress up to the nines and well into double figures. But what is needed for the city as a whole is courageous, inspired investment in design through to the year 2000 and beyond.

We fool ourselves again if we believe British goods are now sufficiently improved in quality, efficiency and looks to beat back the treacherous tide of Continental imports, a tide which will become even more seductive after 1992. Unless our vivid and determined colonies of homegrown designers are to join those émigrés already so prized by Milan, Barcelona, Paris and New York, they require British industry to rustle up enough major and mutually profitable opportunities to detain them proudly at home. Just now there is too much original talent in Glasgow for it to be left pacing up and down in the trap of its own vitality, or – worse still – sent packing into that shrewd embrace of even more hot-shot commercial enemies.

The interior of the Cadoro building – all brass and stained glass.

HUGH COCHRANE

Venice Reclaimed

DONATO BRAMANTE MIGHT HAVE LIKED THE CHALLENGE. RAPHAEL, WHO came later, might have left elegant memorials. They were men who four centuries ago helped to create the latter-day form of Rome, a city, like Glasgow, built on hills around a wayward, undependable river. The place on the Clyde then was scarcely more than a village with little historical, far less geographical, significance, bereft of the material patronage of princes and prelates. Yet at one time it became the Second City of an Empire more vast than that of Rome.

The stone-built Cathedral, replacing one of wood and wattles first raised on the same site about 500 years earlier, was consecrated in 1136. Parts of the original structure remain. The location of it may, for all we know, reflect a measure of religious symbolism as well as the practicality of monks and masons. Towering on a high bluff, it may represent the ways of Kentigern, later Saint Mungo, the patron saint, who, reportedly, when he drew a large crowd, miraculously floated into the air, the better for them to see him.

Glasgow's hills of boulder clay are known as 'drumlins'. Generally, people who had 'made their pile' chose to live on top of these piles. They dwelt well above the river, later above the congested humanity whose homes flanked it and above the smoke and noise of its industries. Terraces, mansions, gardens and wide boulevards survive, mostly in their Victorian form, as testimony to those who went up in the world. Later the city fathers achieved an ironic complementarity when, forced by slum clearance and urban redevelopment, they ringed the city with multi-storey flats for the proletariat, described by a former Chief Planning Officer for Scotland as 'human filing cabinets'. And many were set upon 'drumlins', affording prospects not of the New Jerusalem of socialist planning but of tower blocks on the other side of the city as far as seven or eight miles distant.

Glasgow, from whichever direction it is approached, has fascinating panoramas and skylines, an up-hill-and-down-dale kind of a town, terraced and towered to fit worldly aspirations; it is an urban topography that perhaps appropriately betokens the survival of the fittest – a joytown for young skateboarders but perniciously killing off pensioners, living in council flats on steep streets; statistics in the region reveal a deplorable incidence of coronary and arterial disease.

Economic growth in the late eighteenth and nineteenth centuries was along both banks of the river once that was canalised and maintained by dredging. Discoveries of good coal and blackband ironstone in North Lanarkshire, the development of iron and then steel-hulled ships and international maritime traffic all contributed to that. The city is now Venice Reclaimed. Half a century ago or more it would have been unusual to find a family in the working class or middle class which could not claim some kinsman who had served at sea. The great port, which had flourished in the time of two or three generations, lasted little more than 150 years. Docks where liveried tugboats once escorted cargo ships, ocean liners and the battleships of the fleet in and out of the cramped accesses of berthage were infilled to become

The Templeton Building.

*Scotland Street
School.*

*Central Station
Bridge – newly
painted and
floodlit to
coincide with the
Garden Festival,
1987.*

*Mitchell Library,
Charing Cross.*

*Argyle Street
shopping
precinct, 1986.*

building sites. Only two shipbuilding yards remain where there were more than thirty in the last century.

Along the banks of the now quiet waterway there is disappointingly small evidence of truly coherent and bold planning to raise its asset value, although the many-pavilioned Glasgow Garden Festival of 1988, a prodigous success in terms of attracting visitors, showed what wholesome prettification was possible. The site, on the south bank just west of the Kingston Bridge, has now been cleared for private housing and a portion of parkland. Elsewhere along the river there are new blocks of flats, a few restaurants in converted buildings, offices, a multi-storey hotel and the severely functional Scottish Exhibition and Conference Centre. However, there are also dilapidated, old wharfside sheds, scrap metal yards and other eyesores. If the chance of bringing to the riverside a new graciousness with buildings of similar scale and congruity has not been totally neglected, it certainly appears to be receding fast.

A superb, early example of urban planning is to be seen in the stately terraces above Kelvingrove. Designed by Charles Wilson more than 130 years ago, they represent the strength and dignity which has conferred on Glasgow the accolade of the finest Victorian city in Britain. Across the River Kelvin and mounted on another bluff stands the main building of Glasgow University, a Gothic showpiece by Sir Giles Gilbert Scott. Lord Reith, the first director-general of the BBC and a formidably Gothic figure himself, recalled how as a young man he had stood on the Wilson terraces, gazing over to the University on windy, winter nights and had pondered his destiny.

Glasgow has come to appreciate more fully its Victorian heritage in the past quarter of a century. An end to air pollution (mainly industrial) plus a combined drive by the civic administration and private enterprise to clean, preserve and even floodlight handsome, old buildings have helped to give the people a new vision of their city. A stranger, walking through the centre of it, must frequently look upward; it is essential to enjoy visually the quality of such buildings, particularly their decorative and sculptured tarradiddles that convey the vigour and self-confidence of the prosperous Victorians. If they wanted artwork à la Paris or more than just an architectural memento of Venice, then, by George, they were prepared to scatter a 'wheen o' bawbees' to their architects to get it. Good architects they were, too; mostly Scotsmen with eclectic tastes but who had original ideas of their own and good, local stone with which to implement them.

Flights into eccentricity were relatively few but memorable. Notable among these, the large carpet factory (now the Templeton Business Centre) on the north flank of Glasgow Green, was commissioned by entrepreneurs from the architect, William Leiper, a man best known for his villas and churches. They asked him: 'What is the most beautiful building in the world?' and when he adjudged that to be the Doge's Palace in Venice they said: 'Build it here.' Thus there is his strange, rabbit-warrened replica in terra cotta, red brick and coloured mosaic.

Another item of late Victorian braggadocio with Venetian pretensions is the central tower of the City Chambers in George Square, gazing westwards towards a maritime Rialto that no longer exists. Symbolically, that applies to the Venetian touches of the original part of the Stock Exchange in Buchanan Street too.

Only within the last generation or two has the city been committing its best efforts to preserving the better nineteenth-century buildings in the central area. Part of that drive has been devoted to re-populating

*Kibble Palace,
Botanic Gardens,
1987.*

Botanic Gardens,
Glasgow, 1939.

*Sauchiehall
Street, 1936.*

*Sauchiehall
Street, 1957.*

*Park Circus with
Trinity College
tower and Park
Church in the
background,
1989.*

*Argyle Street –
The Hielan
Man's Umbrella,
looking east from
Oswald Street,
1976.*

*Aerial view of the
new Royal
Scottish
Academy of
Music and
Drama, 1987.*

the Merchant City, roughly identifiable as the zone between the Clyde and George Street, by attracting people to live in new flats or converted warehouses where the lords of the bygone tobacco and textiles trades once dwelt as well as dealt. Although the success of this effort has yet to be proven, the admirable impetus of it is unmistakable. Life there is more varied and lively than it was even twenty years ago. Ironically, its eventual fate could be determined by changing social pressures or retail trading developments just as it did when the merchants and their minions in the eighteenth and early nineteenth centuries enjoyed 'a' the comforts o' the Saltmarket'.

Glasgow has for the first time in many years been indulging itself in new buildings that have not been prompted by purely commercial dictates. The new Royal Scottish Academy of Music and Drama, near to the Theatre Royal, refurbished home of Scottish Opera, is designed not only to nourish the arts and education but also to provide them with the most modern, multi-media facilities for their transmission. Saint Mungo, the patron saint, who proclaimed: 'Let Glasgow flourish by the preaching of the word . . .' was somewhat theatrical in his own behaviour and his ghost (in one of the outer colleges of sainthood) may take marginal pleasure in the strong propagation of music and theatre that has qualified his big, thrusting parish for the honour of being European City of Culture 1990.

Both of these centres of artistic excellence are sited just to the north of one of the main thoroughfares, Sauchiehall Street, which, traditionally, has been considered 'uptown' as distinct from Argyle Street, at a lower, southern level, which is usually deemed 'downtown', is more raffishly commercial and offers all kinds of merchandise and fast foods for the bargain-hungry. The most obvious shopping-thoroughfare link between the two is Buchanan Street, which is well-filled with architectural fascinations and should be the gentle, downhill mall *par excellence.*

Development or enhancement so far has favoured the lower end, although at the upper the provision of the new Glasgow Concert Hall may be a key element in restoring a balance at least. The greater commercial pull of the lower end, notably the elegantly re-appointed Princes Square, opposite Fraser's department store, may represent a Pyrrhic victory, verging upon a Philistine victory because the St Enoch Centre in the square of that name is a gross glasshouse of over-large, uneven design, giving the impression that at one stage its growing panes had to be artificially inhibited for its own, ultimate good.

Every city, of course, contains architectural gaffes, usually not the ancient but the modern. The Anderston Centre, a raised shopping precinct and three blocks of flats on top of a functionally maladroit bus station in which the vehicles have to reverse out of most berths, is a concrete lampoon. Only a couple of streets away on the magnificent Mercantile Chambers (1897) there are sculpted keystone heads which betoken dread and loathing as if they had anticipated the architectural trashmongering of nearby Argyle Street in later generations. The man who designed that building was James Salmon Jun, a contemporary and friend of Charles Rennie Mackintosh whose renowned Glasgow School of Art looms over Sauchiehall Street. Further along the same street, in Henderson's jewellers, there is a recreation of Mackintosh's Willow Tea Rooms with his subtly gracious furniture, textiles and decorations in his version of art nouveau, exemplification of which has become a Glasgow industry.

In Victorian times when an essayist described the city as 'a very Tokyo for tea rooms', the pioneers of municipal socialism, conscious of the growth

Princes Square,
1989.

181

*Smudge, the
well-known
People's Palace
cat, inspects the
renovated Winter
Gardens, 1987.*

of population density, were lavish in the lay-out and maintenance of public parks, green islands amid the onward-marching waves of tenements. They vary wonderfully in size and character. There are parks that would compliment Bath and parks little more than bird baths. There are parks with statues, parks with open-air theatres, parks with squirrels and swans – and even one with an expensive Chinese restaurant in the middle. 'Let Glasgow flourish . . .' said Saint Mungo, and they keep trying with walkways and ceremonial gardens to offer a new, spruce green place. Trees; everywhere, trees in a silviculturist's census that would shame most other cities.

Glaswegians may have become blasé about these parks. One of the most modern adornments, however, has captured world-wide attention as well as their own appreciation. In 1967, Mrs Anne Maxwell Macdonald gifted Pollok Estate on the south side of the city and in it, close to a magnificent Adam House, the Burrell Gallery was built for £20.6 million. It was chosen as winner of an architectural competition to house, in accordance with a somewhat pedantic deed of gift by Sir William Burrell, shipowner, one of the world's finest private collections of paintings, sculpture, tapestries, stained glass, furniture and carpets.

The building, opened by the Queen in 1983, is an artwork in itself, comparable with the best of modernity in the USA, France, West Germany and Japan. Juxtaposition with the Adam house, which itself holds Goyas, El Grecos and examples of some of the most acclaimed, modern British painters, somehow betokens the bridge between the prosperity and confidence of the eighteenth and nineteenth centuries and the best of today's cultural vitality. Culture, in the sense of refinement and the narcissistic glow of self-adornment by societies, can never be largely homogeneous in any city, lest it be content to be seen as a living museum. All things change and Glasgow, through the rises and falls of trading and industrial fortunes, has adapted relatively better than most cities in Europe.

If anyone wished to take away a picture of buildings that reflected good use of its local materials, its architectural skills and the way in which it combined them to overcome problems of population-crowding, it should not be of mansions, churches or mighty institutions but of well-proportioned, durable terraced houses and sandstone tenements with smart adornments of plasterwork and painted glass, the kind which only within the last twenty-five years has the city thought fit to preserve decently. They are strongly typical, especially in the West end and the South side. An unmistakable, intrinsic Glasgow style still lives in the best of them and, for good or ill, it informs all things cultural in the media about this community of Saint Mungo's motley mob.

HARRY REID

Envoi:
Outside Perceptions
of Glasgow

WRITING SIXTY YEARS AGO, THE NOVELIST LEWIS GRASSIC GIBBON DESCRIBED Glasgow as 'the vomit of a cataleptic commercialism'. Having thought about it for a year or so, in 1934 he went further. He wrote of people eating and sleeping and copulating and conceiving and crawling into childhood, 'in those waste jungles of stench and disease and hopelessness, sub-humans as definitely as the Morlocks of Wells – and without even the consolation of feeding on their oppressors' flesh.'

This somewhat extravagant literary treatment of the perceived horrors of Glasgow's slums was by no means untypical of how Glasgow was presented to the world fifty and sixty years ago. In 1935 *No Mean City* was published. It was written by Alexander McArthur and 'tidied up' by H. Kingsley Long, a journalist. It is the best known Glasgow novel, the most notorious and the most commercially successful. It is still selling steadily today.

There had been other 'gangland' novels before *No Mean City* – George Blake's unfortunately titled debut *Mince Collop Close* is an early example – but the success of *No Mean City* spawned a tiresome shoal of even shoddier imitations. A typical case in point is John McNeillie's *Glasgow Keelie*, which came out in 1940.

But *No Mean City* was at once the best and the worst of the Glasgow slum school of fiction, and its influence and potency can hardly be under-estimated. It was presented by its publishers in 1935 as 'a terrible story of drink, poverty, moral corruption and brutality, of the activities of the razor gangs and thugs, against a grim background of tenements, dance halls and cinemas.' A later edition stated: 'When this novel first appeared, it was hailed as the most outspoken novel of the century and it bears every imprint of an enduring masterpiece of documentation – significant, devastating and with a squalid fascination that never palls.'

McArthur and Long were aware of the furore that their novel would cause; in an appendix, they denied that they had exaggerated conditions in the Glasgow tenements. They supported this with a spray of references to stories in the *Daily Record*, the *Evening Times* and the *Sunday Mail* – but not the *Glasgow Herald* – about razor slashings and gangsterdom.

Glasgow then, was presented as a city of slums, of helplessness and of chronic violence. It was also, supremely, regarded as a city of drinkers and drunks. When it came to drinking, sentimentality took over from exaggerated realism. Drinking and violence were rarely linked. Will Fyffe's song of course reflects the acme of this sentimentality:

> I belong to Glasgow
> Dear old Glasgow toon
> But what's the matter wi Glasgow
> For it's going roon and roon.

A more downbeat approach to Glasgow drinking was adopted later by Hugh MacDiarmid in his mischievous essay 'The Dour Drinkers of

183

*Glasgow
holiday-makers
experience their
first sunny day
and stream down
to peg a space on
the beach.*

Rangers supporters, 1977.

Hugh MacDiarmid

Peter Manuel, 1958.

Glasgow'. Although he quoted the Fyffe song, his theme was unsentimental (or perhaps it would be better to say invertedly sentimental). Thus: 'The majority of Glasgow pubs are for connoisseurs of the morose, for those who relish the element of degradation in all boozing and do not wish to have it eliminated by the introduction of music, modernistic fitments, arty effects, or any other extraneous devices whatsoever. It is the old story of those who prefer hard-centre chocolates to soft, storm to sunshine, sour to sweet.'

Here MacDiarmid conveys the no-nonsense hardness, or the would-be hardness, of Glasgow. Yet once again there is literary overkill. Dour drinkers are – and were – in fact much more likely to be found in the pubs of Aberdeen, Dundee or Edinburgh. Glasgow's drinkers tend to be matey and gregarious, even if their friendliness is sometimes charged with suspicion and menace. Once again, we are dealing with exaggeration, mischief-making and myth-making; a syndrome from which Glasgow, more than any other British city, has suffered. But if you dared to criticise the myth-makers, you found that a neat trap had been set. For Glasgow did have slums and hard men and violence; and surely it was right and proper that the city's desperate problems should be ventilated?

* * *

I was born in Glasgow but my family moved to Aberdeen when I was four. During my childhood in Aberdeen in the fifties, I was constantly aware of Glasgow; it was always at the back, sometimes at the front, of my mind, a big, dirty, warm, different place, not so much a dear green place but more of a huge black place, though a special place, the place whence I had come. I remember car journeys down to visit my grandmother in Cambuslang. Scotland changed around Denny and Dunipace. The country seemed to stop. The buildings became dirtier, the roads became busier. The drive from Stepps across to Shettleston and then through the steelworks and up the hill to Cambuslang was at once frightening and magical. I loved Aberdeen and was very happy there; but I was conscious as a child, whenever I was in or around Glasgow, that Aberdeen seemed by comparison too small, too clean, too sterile. Glasgow was teeming, lively and magnificent, in a slightly dangerous, dodgy sort of way.

In Aberdeen, Glasgow was viewed with a mixture of fascination, respect and horror. To some extent Aberdeen was run by Glaswegians, or people from round about Glasgow: the director of education, the medical officer of health, the town clerk, the sheriff clerk, the rector of the grammar school, the principal of the college of education, among others – all came from Glasgow or its environs. These people evinced a certain ambivalence about Glasgow. But there was far more knowledge of, and interest in, Glasgow than Edinburgh. The capital was vaguely perceived as aloof, cold, irrelevant. It was not discussed. Whereas even in Aberdeen, that most serenely self-confident of cities, Glasgow was discussed, and often. Sometimes it was discussed because of news items, or because of the annual league visits of Rangers and Celtic. Their supporters did not behave well, and there was a special pleasure when they were beaten by the Dons, as they frequently were. But the arrival of Rangers, or Celtic, in town was an event, and a big one. Hearts and Hibs and their supporters crept into town and crept out and were hardly noticed.

And in those days, every summer, for the fortnight of the Fair, Glaswegian holidaymakers took over Aberdeen. They complained about the cold, and they mocked the Aberdonian accent, but they enjoyed themselves. When

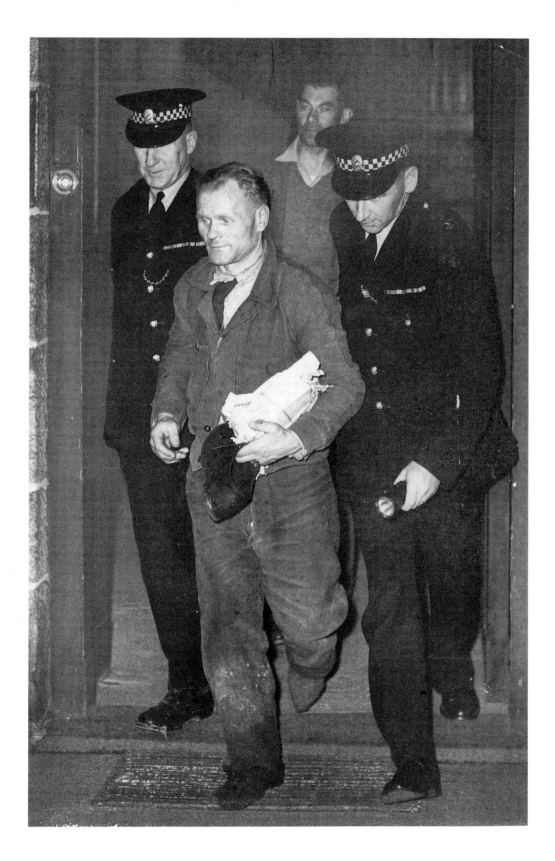

*John Ramensky,
safe-blower and
escapologist.*

I went to live in Edinburgh I observed how a huge influx of visitors transformed the city every summer, during the three weeks of the Festival; yet these thousands of visitors never evinced the cheek, the cocksure *joie de vivre*, the special impertinent friendliness, of the Glasgow folk when they came to Aberdeen.

Then the Glaswegians disappeared, as suddenly as they had arrived, and the rhythm of Aberdeen life recovered its normal steady beat. For a fortnight, the city had been a more colourful and a more chancy place. Now, once again, the mythology, the mystery of Glasgow and Glaswegians, would be picked over. Some young people in Aberdeen seriously believed that if they were brave enough to take the train to Buchanan Street and – even braver – get off it, they would, at best, be assailed by drunks, and, at worst, knifed or shot by gangsters. In reality they might have crossed the road to the Pittodrie Bar (now long since gone) which was a plain, douce wee pub cynically designated to attract the custom of ingenuous Aberdonians. In any event, it allowed Aberdonians the comfort of a friendly arrival or a sentimental departure. There were many tougher bars in Aberdeen's docklands. But we are dealing here with the potency of myths, with the perceptions of a city filtered through bad literature, worse journalism and music-hall sentimentality. And, from time to time, news stories provided a spectacular and grainy endorsement of such perceptions.

The Manuel Trial in 1958 was the supreme example; it was a godsend to those who made it their business to perpetrate a certain vision of the underside of Glasgow. Manuel himself was a one-off: a mass murderer, a psychopath, a native not of Glasgow but of Manhattan, an avid consumer of gangster novels, a man of no education but exceptionally well-schooled in petty crime, an ignorant, cocky man with supreme forensic skills (he should have been a lawyer), as was proved when he dismissed his distinguished counsel and conducted his own defence with quite remarkable cunning. The trial was dramatic; at its climax Manuel, in the dock, questioned a Glasgow businessman in a wheelchair, each accusing the other of the same murders.

But as far as extraneous perceptions of Glasgow were concerned, it was undoubtedly the incidental evidence that proved most potent. There was a great deal about pubs and sustained drinking bouts, about an illegal gambling school on the banks of the Clyde run by a sinister figure called Totten and sometimes attended by as many as 300 punters, about the casual buying and selling of guns in the Glasgow underworld, of petty criminals easing in and out of Barlinnie prison and running errands for larger, yet darker figures.

Take one minor episode: Totten, who ran the gambling school, had asked a witness, Fullerton, to get him a weapon. Fullerton was in a pub one evening when a man approached him and asked him if he could use a gun, a loaded Beretta. Fullerton at once paid a deposit of £1. Totten then gave him £6, £5 for the gun and £1 for commission.

The evidence in the Manuel trial was pored over by people throughout Scotland, and indeed the UK. It seemed to endorse the received wisdom, to give point and detail to the hitherto somewhat imprecise impression of violence and gangsterdom, of hard men and harder living (and dying). To some extent this remains, even now, the conventional image of Glasgow, though there is more sophistication, more craft in the two 'Laidlaw' novels by William McIlvanney, and more sheen and gloss in the unfortunately successful STV series *Taggart*.

But a greater, more positive and more powerful myth now sustains

Glasgow. It is the myth that Glasgow is miles better, and the concomitant perception of Glasgow as a vibrant, enterprising model of a city, a city that has boldly shed the carapace of its dismal past and is now blinking with happy agitation in the bright, blinding dawn of undreamt of civic glory. Well, that's a bit over the top; but then the new, vogue presentation of Glasgow is also a bit over the top. In truth, the new myth would have less relevance if it had not superseded such an unfair, unduly negative old one. And there is no doubt that many aspects of Glasgow's renaissance are very genuine. I have benefited greatly from it myself; it would be hypocritical, ungrateful churlishness to deflate the city's sudden self-delight. Again, so much of what it has had to put up with in the past, the overwritten diatribes, the slanted dissections of its crime and its squalor – Glasgow suffered greatly and unjustly from these, and it deserves its current retribution and redemption, even if these can be a little too slick and too glib for comfort.

Reference has been made earlier in this book to the 'Glasgow's Miles Better' campaign of the early eighties. There can be no doubt, and I assert this with as much categorical conviction as I can muster, that it was one of the best things ever to have been visited on Glasgow. For there can be no denying that there has been a sea-change in the way the rest of the world perceives Glasgow. Teddy Taylor, for many years the MP for Glasgow Cathcart, and for the last ten years the MP for the very different seat of Southend East in south-east England's commuting country, recalls that when he was first there, fighting a by-election, his supporters were embarrassed that he came from Glasgow. 'It was awful. Glasgow was perceived as a gloomy, sad, nasty town that was very far away. Now it is very, very different. Glasgow is perceived as a place of culture, of beauty, even of intellect. Whereas ten years ago Glasgow was thought of as appalling, uncivilised, grim and above all violent, it's now a place that many of my constituents actually want to visit. It has veritably been transformed into a golden city.'

Earlier I wrote about how my own early impressions of Glasgow were filtered through my childhood in the very different city of Aberdeen. The poet G.S. Fraser had a similar background: born in Glasgow, he was taken to live in Aberdeen when he was very young. He wrote that he left Glasgow while the city was only a symbol to him. In his autobiography, *A Stranger and Afraid* – a book that deserves to be much better known – Fraser wrote of Glasgow: 'Yet if there is a kind of horror about Glasgow, there is a kind of cosiness, too . . . It is, unlike London, a neighbourly place . . . Glasgow is provincial in the sense of having failed to become a capital; the great dowdy creature, gathering up her own trailing skirts, has little thought to spare for the rest of Scotland, and for the rest of Scotland also Glasgow is strangely alien.'

I think that is beautifully written, and in a sense true; but even that is slightly unkind to Glasgow, and it does not reflect the new realities. I'm certainly not sure that Glasgow is, any more, strangely alien from the rest of Scotland. Rather, Glasgow has become an emblem, a manifestation of what the rest of Scotland might become. It is a city with guts, of course it is; but it also has plenty of that most pleasing and gentle of all qualities, grace. I hope, in the years to come, that more people – and particularly more people who interpret Glasgow to the rest of the world, will realise this.

Good luck to Glasgow, and God bless it.

Notes on Contributors

ARNOLD KEMP. Editor since 1981. Pursues a passion for politics, economics and Hibernian Football Club. Former Deputy Editor of *The Scotsman*.

HARRY REID. Deputy Editor since 1983, a year after he joined the paper from the *Sunday Standard*. Glasgow born, he returned to the city after other lives in Aberdeen and Edinburgh.

MURRAY RITCHIE. Assistant Editor. A reporter and feature writer on the *Herald* for 18 years he has collected a clutch of awards. Was Scotland's first Journalist of the Year.

JACK WEBSTER. Feature writer and columnist. After travelling the world for the *Scottish Daily Express* he took to writing books about his Aberdeen homeland.

JACK McLEAN. Columnist and feature writer. Described as a 'master wordsmith' when he won the 1989 Scottish Feature Writer of the Year award. A former teacher now in a class of his own.

ALF YOUNG. Economics Editor. Scotland's most authoritative economics journalist. Winner of the Financial/Business Writer of the Year award in the 1989 Bank of Scotland Press Awards.

ANDREW YOUNG. Entertainments Editor. One of the country's foremost voices on theatre and TV affairs.

HUGH COCHRANE. Feature writer and columnist. Former News Editor of BBC Scotland and author of 'Glasgow – The First 800 Years'.

WILLIAM HUNTER. An outstanding observer of the Glasgow scene. After emigrating from Paisley he punctuated a feature-writing career with a spell as the *Herald*'s Business Editor.

JOHN FOWLER. Arts Editor, playwright, critic and vastly experienced guide to Glasgow's arts.

STEWART LAMONT. The *Herald*'s religious affairs columnist. Successful novelist and broadcaster and producer of religious programmes for BBC Scotland.

ANNE SIMPSON. Chief Assistant Editor and Women's Editor. Scotland's leading writer on fashion and style. Far-travelled writer on foreign affairs. Her own writing style has won many awards, including Scotland's Columnist of the year and Specialist Writer.

RAYMOND GARDNER. (Trencherman). Distinctive and distinguished food writer on the *Herald* for 7 years. Winner of the prestigious Glenfiddich Regional Writer of the Year Award in 1987.

ROBERT McLAUGHLAN. The thinking drinker's guru. For 20 years his encyclopedic knowledge of the wine industry has been the basis of the *Herald*'s popular wine column.

IAN PAUL. Stylish sports reporter and outspoken columnist. He has covered major sporting events in Scotland and in Europe for the Herald for 12 years.

DAVID BELCHER. Outspoken and stylish commentator on the turbulent pop world.